Numbers and Stories

Numbers and Stories

*Using Children's Literature to Teach
Young Children Number Sense*

Rita C. Janes

Elizabeth L. Strong

A JOINT PUBLICATION

FOR INFORMATION:

Corwin

A SAGE Company

2455 Teller Road

Thousand Oaks, California 91320

(800) 233-9936

www.corwin.com

SAGE Publications Ltd.

1 Oliver's Yard

55 City Road

London EC1Y 1SP

United Kingdom

SAGE Publications India Pvt. Ltd.

B 1/I 1 Mohan Cooperative Industrial Area

Mathura Road, New Delhi 110 044

India

SAGE Publications Asia-Pacific Pte. Ltd.

3 Church Street

#10-04 Samsung Hub

Singapore 049483

Acquisitions Editor: Robin Najar
Associate Editor: Desirée A. Bartlett
Editorial Assistant: Ariel Price
Production Editors: Laura Barrett and Amy
                    Schroller
Copy Editor: Megan Markanich
Typesetter: C&M Digitals (P) Ltd.
Proofreader: Dennis W. Webb
Indexer: Michael Ferreira
Cover Designer: Scott Van Atta

Copyright © 2014 by Corwin

Printed in the United States of America

A catalog record of this book is available from the Library of Congress.

ISBN 978-1-4833-3094-5

This book is printed on acid-free paper.

14 15 16 17 18 10 9 8 7 6 5 4 3 2 1

Contents

Preface

Many teachers enjoy integrating children's literature throughout all or most curriculum areas. However, when integrating mathematics and children's literature, they ask for support in implementing rich mathematical learning experiences that emanate from the literature and are sufficiently significant and meaningful to meet the learning expectations of the prescribed curriculum standards they are using.

Numbers and Stories: Using Children's Literature to Teach Young Children Number Sense provides instructional support based on what is known from pedagogical research and practice related to integrating meaningfully mathematics and children's literature and to creating purposefully mathematical learning experiences that originate from the literature. The book fosters children's learning of important mathematics in a context that is "robust and relevant to the real world" (Common Core State Standards Initiative [CCSSI], 2012b). In this book such a context is provided mainly through children's literature that relates in a real or fictional manner to their daily experiences.

The purpose of this book is to provide a professional teaching and learning resource to meet the above stated needs of teachers. It is intended for teachers of young children, kindergarten to Grade 2, and professional development consultants. A secondary audience is mentors and coaches, early childhood and primary education professors and students, and school district and department of education curriculum consultants and administrators.

HOW THE BOOK IS ORGANIZED

Numbers and Stories is divided into two parts—Part I: Here's the Story: Fundamental Components for Developing Number Sense Using Children's Literature and Part II: Children's Literature and Number Sense Investigations. Part I, organized into five chapters, presents the design and special features of the instructional approach used in the Investigations (Part II), along with the pedagogical research and knowledge gleaned from best practices that support this approach.

Included in Part II are 21 Investigations, each introduced through a quality mathematics-related children's book depicting the mathematics being explored that is revisited and used as a resource throughout each Investigation. The content of these Investigations focuses on the development of number sense for the young child (kindergarten to Grade 2), with clearly stated learning expectations chosen from the Common Core State Standards (CCSS) for Mathematics (2012b) and in keeping with other mathematics curriculum documents across North America. Besides the mathematics content associated with number sense, the processes of mathematics, such as problem solving, reasoning, communicating, representing, and making connections, are integrated throughout the Investigations. As well, the Investigations include learning expectations from the CCSSI for English Language Arts (2012a) related to literacy—in particular, reading standards for literature, informational text, and foundational skills; writing standards; speaking and listening standards; and language standards.

The Investigations are designed so that children are actively involved, physically and mentally, in rich problem solving tasks that support the development of mathematical understanding and procedures and where children are encouraged to use their own strategies and prior knowledge to find solutions to these tasks. These tasks include well-designed questions throughout to create an inquiry based environment where discourse provides the foundation for learning how to reason mathematically.

The Investigations may be experienced by various groups of children, at various age levels, at various times throughout the school year and may be revisited at any time. There is no set sequential order for their implementation since teachers know their children best and the mathematics they want them to achieve. The Investigations are not meant to be translated standard by standard but more woven as a lattice and "the order of the Standards neither implies a teaching sequence nor sets out connections among ideas in different topics" (CCSSI, 2012b).

SPECIAL FEATURES OF THE BOOK

Carefully Designed, Engaging, Interactive Mathematics Investigations Connected to Common Core State Standards Supported by Research—The learning expectations for the Investigations are selected from the CCSS for Mathematics (CCSSI, 2012b) and the CCSS for English Language Arts (CCSSI, 2012a) for children in kindergarten to Grade 2 (Learning Expectations Correlation Chart, Appendix F). As well, they are correlated with the learning expectations associated with the curriculum standards used in most schools in North America, even if schools have chosen not to use CCSS.

Formative Assessment Throughout Each Investigation—The main assessment tool in the Investigations is observation, providing support and guidance for the teacher while monitoring children's learning. It is intended to determine how well the children are meeting the stated learning expectations as they work actively and in an inquiring manner on the problem solving tasks. It assists also the teacher in being more responsive to and flexible in making appropriate moment-to-moment decisions to meet the children's needs.

Reflection and Discussion Questions and Prompts for Children and Teachers—At the end of each Investigation, questions and prompts are provided to guide children and teachers as they think consciously about and communicate their experiences and feelings while engaged in the Investigation. As the reflections are shared with peers and colleagues, learning is enhanced and teaching is improved to better meet the needs of all children.

Acknowledgments

Writing this professional teaching and learning book evolved slowly over many years. It has been truly a cooperative writing venture that has required immense collaboration and appreciation for each other's professional expertise. However, its completion would not have been possible without the help, support, and encouragement from many people throughout the process.

We are indebted greatly to the Corwin Press team who accepted our manuscript and guided us relentlessly with care and understanding throughout this challenging but rewarding writing journey. After senior acquisition editor Robin Najar read the manuscript she informed us that she saw its potential and endorsed it. We thank her profusely. Ariel Price, editorial assistant, was most patient in guiding us through the editorial stage, making sure our manuscript was properly organized and all the elements were included. We are most grateful to her. And Laura Barrett, production editor, as well as Amy Schroller, project editor guided us reassuringly through each stage of the production process; we are truly grateful to them as well. To all of you and those at Corwin who assisted in any way to make this book become a reality, we thank you.

The reviewers' (Julie Duford, Debra Scarpelli, and Michelle Tavenner) constructive and supportive comments were most helpful and encouraging, providing us guidance as we reviewed and revised continuously our manuscript. We are most appreciative.

FROM RITA

I extend a sincere appreciation to my family, colleagues, teachers, and students that I had the good fortune to share my love of mathematics with over the past 50 years. I am especially grateful that they accompanied me on this incredible journey of teaching, learning, and enjoying mathematics. In particular, I am grateful for experiencing the joy on the faces of children and teachers when they experienced those 'aha' moments while learning and teaching the important mathematics included in the Investigations in this book.

A very special thank-you to Jack and Jacqui, two very special people in my life, who offered so much love, support, and encouragement while writing this book.

I also express my appreciation to the National Council of Teachers of Mathematics (NCTM) community in the United States and Canada. I am grateful for the opportunities provided by serving on the NCTM board and committees but most of all the learning from all the mathematics teachers that I had the pleasure to meet and learn from as a fifty-one-year member of this professional organization.

FROM ELIZABETH

I am most grateful to the many primary and elementary students I have been fortunate to teach and learn from. They demonstrated innately and freely their curiosity and enthusiasm for and engagement in children's books from all literary genres throughout the curriculum. Such joys and involvement in their books inspired me to pursue further studies in the area of children's and adolescent literature. As well, I am deeply thankful to my undergraduate and graduate students who further motivated and challenged me by their eagerness and desire to integrate literature in their curriculum and by sharing their insights related to the importance and power of literature in their students' lives. To all of them, I am sincerely appreciative and hope that they will continue to enjoy and share their compassion for literature with their students and colleagues.

I express also my heartfelt thanks to the teachers and colleagues I have taught with and learned from and those whom I had worked with through professional development. All have demonstrated their commitment and dedication in assisting young children to discover the importance and power of literature in their lives—as well as its value across the curriculum.

My siblings and their families have been instrumental in providing ongoing love, support, and encouragement throughout my educational and professional journeys. Jim (Glenda) Strong, Pearl (Hugh) Grant, and Percy (Jean) Strong have followed me through each stage of my journeys and celebrated each milestone. To them, I am immeasurably grateful. My nieces and nephews—Jennifer (Christian) Hawn, Christina (Scott) Sutton, and Steven (Lorri) Strong; John (Sherry) Grant, Janet (Andrew) Carpenter, and Timothy Grant; and Christopher and Andrew Strong—have shared with me from the youngest of their years their joys and engagement in all genres of literature and the importance of it in their lives. To them, I thank them most sincerely and will support and encourage them as they continue to value literature in their lives and their children's lives.

Publisher's Acknowledgments

Corwin would like to thank the following individuals for taking the time to provide their editorial insight and guidance:

Julie Duford, Fifth Grade Teacher
Polson Middle School
Winner of the 2004 Presidential Award for Teaching Elementary Mathematics
Polson, MT

Debra Scarpelli, Math Teacher
Slater Jr. High School
Pawtucket, RI

Michelle Tavenner, Teacher
Gahanna-Jefferson Public Schools
Gahanna, OH

About the Authors

Rita C. Janes has spent a lifetime as a teacher. She taught at all levels of schooling, including the teaching of mathematics and mathematics education for preservice teachers. She served as a mathematics professional development consultant at the district level with responsibilities from kindergarten to Grade 12. In recent years she has been facilitating workshops on mathematics instruction with teachers and school districts across Canada and the United States. She has a special interest in supporting teachers as they strive to integrate the National Council of Teachers of Mathematics (NCTM) Process Standards and the CCSS for Mathematical Practice into the content of elementary mathematics programs, helping to make these programs come alive in the classroom.

Rita promotes the use of rich problem solving tasks, mathematical discourse, and the posing of good questions to ensure inquiry-oriented classroom environments for all children. Observing how young children are more successful learners of mathematics when it is presented in a familiar context, she finds great success in using children's literature as this context.

Rita has served on the board of directors of the National Council of Supervisors of Mathematics (NCSM); the the board of directors of the NCTM; chair of the NCTM Professional Development Services Committee; chair of the NCTM Affiliate Services Committee; member of the NCTM Educational Services Committee; president of Newfoundland and Labrador Teachers' Association (NLTA) Mathematics Council; president of the NLTA Elementary Teachers' Council; and editor of *Teaching Mathematics* (an NLTA publication).

Elizabeth L. Strong is first and foremost a teacher. Her career began as a primary–elementary teacher, then elementary school administrator, school district primary education coordinator, and university professor. Elizabeth's professional journey has focused mainly on literacy, language arts, and children's literature. She has been and continues to be an international, national, provincial, and regional professional development presenter and facilitator of topics related to these areas. However, as of late, her main focus is using effectively children literature in the classroom to encourage young children to discover and explore the delights in books of all genres and to support, extend, and enrich all areas of the curriculum.

Elizabeth has served on the International Board on Books for Young Children; the Canadian Children's Book Centre: Our Choice Committee; the Prime Minister's Awards for Teaching Excellence in Science, Technology, and Mathematics Committee; and Canadian Association for Young Children. She has been a member of the *Journal of the Early Childhood Education Council,* the College of the North Atlantic Early Childhood Education Committee, the International Reading Association, and a member of and reviewer for the *Journal of the National Council of Teachers of English,* as well as the president of the Newfoundland and Labrador Teachers' Association (NLTA) Reading Council.

PART I

Here's the Story: Fundamental Components for Developing Number Sense Using Children's Literature

1 The Young Child and Mathematics

WHY MATHEMATICS FOR YOUNG CHILDREN?

Young children live in a world permeated with mathematics. When they play in the sandbox, pour water, sort forks and knives, build with blocks, count steps as they walk up stairs, collect leaves, and share their toys, they are measuring, sorting, counting, noticing shapes and patterns, and making fair shares. These everyday experiences along with their natural curiosity and enthusiasm for learning provide the foundation for children's mathematical development.

Besides the mathematics children experience everywhere in their lived world, their more formal mathematics, such as reasoning, problem solving, spatial visualization, identification of patterns and relationships are valued for further education and in society (Van de Walle, 2003). It is the gateway to many careers, such as medicine, engineering, architecture, computer science, economics, social sciences, and other areas not usually associated with mathematics, such as the fine arts and interior design.

Often children do not recognize that mathematics is all around them, but with adult support, they can come to appreciate that mathematics is a common human activity that plays a major role in their lives and helps them make sense of their lived world.

LEARNING MATHEMATICS IN THE EARLY YEARS

Preschool Years

It is during the preschool years that the foundation for mathematical development is established. Based on everyday experiences, formal and informal, children develop a rather complex set of informal ideas about numbers, patterns, shapes, quantities, data, and size (National Council of Teachers of Mathematics [NCTM], 2000, p. 21). Kilpatrick, Swafford, and Findell (2001) confirm this by saying, "Starting from infancy and continuing throughout the preschool period, [children] develop a base of skills, concepts, and misconceptions" (p. 5). The informal mathematics that children experience in the early years is analogous to how they learn to speak. Just as one learns to talk—and spoken language is a foundation of reading—so one develops an informal mathematics that serves as the foundation for the more abstract mathematics they learn in school (Ginsburg & Baron, 1993, p. 3).

Early School Years

"At no time in schooling is cognitive growth so remarkable" (NCTM, 2000, p. 76) as during the first years of formal schooling, prekindergarten to Grade 2. In this regard, such growth in mathematics, as stated in the Learning Principle (NCTM, 2000), depends on the children learning mathematics with understanding, actively building new knowledge from experience and prior knowledge. They do this by building and extending on their informal mathematical learning and on their enthusiasm and curiosity from their preschool years. It is well recognized in the literature that children develop this understanding of mathematics by being actively involved, physically and mentally, in their own learning, trying "to make sense of methods and explanations they see or hear from others" (Yackel, Cobb, Wood, Wheatley, & Merkel, 1990, p. 13).

2 The Learning Environment

Imagine a [learning environment] . . . where all [children] have access to high quality, engaging mathematics instruction. The curriculum is mathematically rich, offering [children] opportunities to learn important mathematical concepts and procedures with understanding. Alone or in groups, they work productively and reflectively, with the skilled guidance of their teachers. Orally and in writing [and other ways of representing, children] communicate their ideas and results effectively. They value mathematics and engage actively learning it. (National Council of Teachers of Mathematics [NCTM], 2000, p. 3)

FEATURES OF THE LEARNING ENVIRONMENT

An effective, supportive learning environment that ensures young children will be actively and successfully involved in learning mathematical content and processes includes the following features. They are elaborated on in the succeeding sections and are embedded in each Investigation in this book.

- Rich problem solving tasks
- Productive discourse opportunities
- Learning resources
- Differentiated learning experiences
- Observation of children's learning

Rich Problem Solving Tasks

Children achieve the learning expectations stated for an Investigation by being actively involved, physically and mentally, in finding solutions to rich problem solving tasks. These tasks may not have a prescribed or learned way of finding a solution, but children are encouraged to use their own strategies and prior knowledge to do so (Common Core State Standards Initiative [CCSSI], 2012a; NCTM, 2000). Furthermore, since developing mathematical understanding and procedures are both very important they can be developed as stated in CCSSI (2012a), "by using mathematical tasks of sufficient richness."

The problem solving tasks are developed in keeping with the idea expressed by Hiebert (2003), "allowing mathematics to be problematic does not mean making mathematics unnecessarily difficult, but it does mean allowing [children] to wrestle with what is mathematically challenging" (p. 55). In creating these tasks the authors heeded the caution of Van de Walle (2003): "tasks that are too easy offer little opportunity for growth. Tasks too far out of reach can frustrate [children] and 'turn them off'" (p. 73). When children are given well-designed problem solving tasks, they construct, revise, and refine their mathematical understandings to make sense of and solve the problems (Battista, 2002, p. 75).

Productive Discourse Opportunities

There are many integrated opportunities throughout the Investigations for children and teachers to engage in productive discourse. Productive discourse is referred in *Mathematics Teaching Today* as "ways of representing, thinking, talking, agreeing, and disagreeing" (NCTM, 2007, p. 46) and implies having an awareness of and respect for the perspectives, reasoning, solution strategies, and ideas of others.

Productive discourse involves first allowing children to "construct arguments using concrete referents such as objects, drawings, diagrams, and actions" (CCSSI, 2012a) and then providing an environment where children can explain their ideas and justify solutions through spoken, written, and visual language. *However, it is more than that.* It is the dynamics that happen between children and children and also between children and teacher— where everyone listens to the ideas of others and feels safe to challenge these ideas if they are not fully understood or are of a different opinion, always recognizing that mathematical reasoning and evidence are the basis for discourse (NCTM, 2000) and "mathematically proficient students . . . justify their conclusions, communicate to others, and respond to arguments of others" (CCSSI, 2012a).

In order for productive discourse to be an essential part of the learning environment, the following were given considerable attention throughout the Investigations:

- Role of questioning
- Role of listening
- Opportunities to generalize
- Grouping for instruction
- Risk-free environment

Role of Questioning

Well-posed questions are essential in stimulating productive discourse in the classroom and are the foundation for learning how to reason mathematically. Questions asked by the teacher must invite and challenge children to think deeply about the mathematical idea under discussion, as well, "foster in-depth inquiry, a necessary component of deeply structured learning" (Booth, 1998, p. 76). As children share solutions to questions they are extending their own mathematical knowledge and problem solving strategies, while becoming more aware of their own reasoning and sense making of the mathematics they are learning. This enhances learning for all, as long as the sharing among children focuses on children's "methods for constructing solutions, not simply on their answers to the problem" (NCTM, 2000, p. 52).

Besides the teacher posing questions, the children, too, are encouraged to pose questions. This requires them to think deeply about the mathematics in the task at hand, developing their higher order skills and important mathematics. Teachers have to consider carefully the kinds of questions children ask and what they are telling them about their mathematical understanding. They can give valuable insights into children's reasoning.

The teacher orchestrates the discourse by asking the following types of questions and prompts, helping all children become members of a productive discourse community and move forward in their reasoning about the mathematical ideas being considered:

- Tell us more about why your answer shows thirty.
- Did anyone do it differently? Tell us about it.
- Do you agree with what she said? Tell us why.
- Can someone tell us why Tomi thought about it that way?
- Do you understand what she just said? Maybe you can show us with the blocks.
- Does this group have a question they would like to ask?
- Now does it make more sense to you? Why?
- Have you seen a problem like this before?
- What happens if . . . ?
- Can you state a general rule for what you found?

Role of Listening

Productive discourse requires children and teachers to be attentive listeners. There is an expectation that sharing solutions to questions is not sufficient but children must analyze each other's solutions. When children are involved actively in analyzing solutions presented by peers, rather than waiting for the teacher to tell them if they are right or wrong, their abilities to think critically are greatly enhanced (NCTM, 2007). For this to happen, children must learn to listen attentively so that they can ask for clarifications and ask questions in order to make sense of the responses of peers (NCTM, 2000).

Teaching is often described as listening. Teachers have an important role in being attentive and active listeners. In order to ask the follow-up questions to the one they originally asked they have to listen attentively to what children say and do. Yackel (2003) maintains that "First we must hear what they say. Second, we need to make sense of what they say and do" (p. 113). Throughout the Investigations, a number of questions related to the tasks is suggested to support the teacher in furthering the children's learning.

Opportunities to Generalize

After a solution to a problem is found and shared, an important step is to look at the solution and determine if it can be generalized. "Generalization is the strategy of identifying a pattern of information or events and using the pattern to formulate conclusions about other like situations" (Small, Sheffield, Cavanagh, Dacey, L., Findell, & Greenes, 2004, p.2). Several of the problem solving tasks in this book challenge children to make generalizations in informal ways by examining drawings and looking for patterns in recorded data.

Investigation Connection

One Big Building: A Counting Book About Construction (Dahl, 2005) Investigation—A series of follow-up questions is used to challenge children to make a generalization about any number of tires on the truck illustrated in the book:

- If there were four trucks, how many tires would there be? How do you know?
- What if we had five trucks?
- Could you tell how many if you had ten trucks? How do you know?
- Could you tell how many tires if you had any number of trucks? How do you know?

Finding a solution to these questions and making a generalization about any number of trucks is the foundation of algebraic reasoning for these young children.

Grouping for Instruction

The authors believe that children learn best in a learning environment where there is a community of learners making sense of mathematical ideas in a climate of collaboration and productive discourse. There can be various learning structures to allow for collaborative productive discourse. In this book, tasks are organized so that children are working sometimes with partners and small groups, sometimes with whole groups, sometimes at centers, and sometimes individually where they know they can call on the expertise of peers when necessary and in all cases under the guidance and support of a teacher or another adult. Different arrangements are suggested in this book but as with the execution of all learning tasks with young children, teachers have to be flexible in organizing learning to best suit the different needs of the children (NCTM, 2007). Hence, whatever the grouping arrangement, the purpose is to develop mathematical understanding and skills, make conjectures, test ideas, and create arguments where the contributions of all children in the community are valued.

Risk-Free Environment

Children require a learning environment that "fosters intellectual growth and development" (NCTM, 2007, p. 45), where they learn to question with respect the ideas and thinking of peers, along with justifying their own reasoning and answering questions asked of them without becoming hostile or defensive (NCTM, 2001). When this type of risk-free environment is nurtured by the teacher, children "become confident in their ability to tackle difficult problems, eager to figure things out on their own, flexible in exploring mathematical ideas and trying alternative solution paths, and willing to persevere" (NCTM, 2000, p. 21).

Learning Resources

Teachers and children have many learning resources available to help them make sense of the mathematics they are teaching and learning. The following are elaborated on, as they are the ones more specifically named throughout the Investigations: children's literature, manipulatives—concrete, manipulatives—virtual, and presentation tools.

Children's Literature

Noted English poet and novelist, the late Walter de la Mare (1942), in reference to books for children, asserts, "Only the rarest kind of best in anything can be good enough for the young" (p. 9). This statement is as relevant to the books selected for young children today as it was then. It is also pertinent to the selection of mathematics-related children's books used to foster today's young children's mathematical understandings.

Quality mathematics-related children's books engage, entertain, and inspire children and appeal to their various interests. They are multilayered, spanning a range of thinking levels . . . . (Morrow & Gambrell, 2004). The selection of the best of the best is dependent on the use of evaluative criteria related to each book's literary genre and mathematical perspective. Kiefer, Hepler, and Hickman (2007) maintain the criteria used to evaluate a book vary according to its literary genre. For example, in picture storybooks "the verbal text and illustrations interact harmoniously," while in nonfiction books the information must be "accurate and unbiased" (pp. 14–15).

The children's books selected for this book are mainly from the picture book genre. The major types of books chosen from this genre are picture storybooks and concept books.

Manipulatives—Concrete

Manipulative materials, sometimes referred to in the literature as concrete materials, models, or tools, are integrated throughout the Investigations. The suggested manipulatives for learning and teaching number sense are counters of all sorts, base ten blocks, linking cubes, number cards, and 5- and 10-Frames.

Manipulative materials are supports for children to explore and make sense of mathematical ideas—but only if the children actually handle and manipulate them. They are often thought of as a representation for a concept. However, when children look at a manipulative, all they can see is the manipulative. It is their minds that impose the mathematical relationship on the materials. Hiebert (2003) states that "meaning is not inherent in the tool; [children] construct meaning for it" (p. 55). They construct that meaning only if they are the ones that manipulate the materials. These learning resources, referred to as tools in CCSSI (2012a), should be sufficiently familiar to children at their grade level "to make sound decisions about when each of these tools might be useful, recognizing both the insight to be gained and their limitations" (p. 2). It is important to distinguish whether children need manipulatives to solve a problem successfully or rely on manipulatives to solve a problem that they could solve in other ways.

Manipulatives—Virtual

Presently, virtual manipulatives are available on the web as teaching and learning tools. They can either be static or dynamic. Static manipulatives—for example, pictures on a screen—are ones that children cannot move or manipulate. However, dynamic manipulatives are very similar to the 'hands on' manipulatives described above but are web-based representations of these materials. They can be moved around on the computer screen by means of a computer mouse or key, allowing children to construct meaning of mathematical ideas on their own by actually moving the objects with slides, flips, or turns (Moyer, Bolyard, & Spikell, 2002).

Teachers wonder often about the merits of dynamic virtual manipulatives as compared to actual concrete ones young children can hold in their hands. In this regard Clements (1999), based on experiences of using virtual manipulatives with young children, states the following:

> Good manipulatives are those that are meaningful to the learner; provide control and flexibility to the learner; have characteristics that mirror, or are consistent with, cognitive and mathematics structures; and assist the learner in making connections between various pieces and types of knowledge—in a word, serving as a catalyst for the growth of integrated—concrete knowledge. Computer manipulatives can serve the function.

Presentation Tools

Permeating the tasks in each Investigation, children are expected to present their solutions to their peers, whether working independently or in groups using the traditional presentation tools, such as paper and pencil, recording sheets, chart paper, chalkboards, or overhead projectors. However, if electronic presentation tools are available in the learning environment, such as word processing, PowerPoint, document readers, and interactive electronic boards, they can easily be incorporated into any of the Investigations.

Differentiated Learning Experiences

Problem tasks throughout the Investigations allow for multiple solutions and strategies. When problems can be solved in more than one way, there are multiple entry points for children who may be working at different levels, hence making the problems more accessible for all children and easier for teachers to differentiate the learning experiences for them.

However, no matter how rich and well laid out the problem solving tasks are presented in books and resource guides for teachers, at times they are not sufficient for meeting the needs of all children. The teacher still has to decide how that task will be used to suit the varied levels of knowledge, abilities, and interests of each child. Observation of the children as they pursue the different tasks in an Investigation is very important. As NCTM (2007) states, "Teachers must . . . decide what aspects of a task to highlight, how to organize and orchestrate the work . . . [and] what questions to ask to challenge those with varied levels of expertise" (p. 23). Even though the authors of this book have laid out a sequence of steps and questions to direct a particular task, the teacher, having observed the children's responses, has to be flexible in how an Investigation may continue to best elicit and extend their mathematical understanding. Finding a balance between managing the Investigation according to children's needs and focusing the discussion on the learning trajectory planned originally is often a challenge and does require a lot of skill (Smith & Stein, 2011).

Observation of Children's Learning

It is known widely that young children know more than they are able to express in writing and speaking (NCTM, 2000) or other ways of representing. Therefore, to be truly informed about children's knowledge, teachers use a variety of assessments, such as observations, oral presentations, interviews, work samples, portfolios, and journals.

The main assessment tool in the Investigations is observation, providing support and guidance for the teacher while monitoring the children's learning. It is not intended for summative evaluation purposes but rather to determine how well the children are meeting the stated learning expectations as they work actively and in an inquiring manner on the problem solving tasks in each Investigation. They are intended also to assist the teacher in being more responsive to and flexible in making appropriate moment-by-moment decisions to meet the children's needs.

Investigation Connection

Balancing Act (Walsh, 2010)/*Equal Shmequal* (Kroll, 2005) Investigation—The following questions are suggested to help teachers observe the children's learning:

- What counting strategies do the children use to match the dominoes?
- Are children fluent in writing the corresponding equation for the matching dominoes?
- Can they explain why the two dominoes are equivalent?
- How fluent and confident are they in finding the missing numbers in the equations? Are some formats more challenging than others?
- What strategies do they use to find the missing numbers?

Teachers know that by carefully observing children they are in a better position to make decisions about the appropriate follow-up learning experiences children require.

SUMMARY

The importance of an effective, supportive learning environment that ensures young children will be actively and successfully involved in learning mathematical content and processes is well recognized. This chapter describes the considerations for a learning environment to enhance the mathematical learning experiences for young children, considered in designing the Investigations in Part II of this book.

3 Why Integrate Children's Literature and Mathematics?

CHILDREN'S LITERATURE AND LEARNING MATHEMATICS

Children's literature creates within young children an *inward* or *intrinsic* experience that helps them to gain a sense of connection to their lived world (Vandergrift, 1986, p. 1), assisting them in making sense of their lives and the world around them. This is so, as they encounter mathematical understandings through various literary genres—for example, fiction, nonfiction, and poetry. They make connections and interrelationships, bringing meaning to the mathematics in their lives. It is for this reason and others to follow that credence is given for integrating children's literature and mathematics throughout each Investigation in this book.

REASONS FOR INTEGRATING CHILDREN'S LITERATURE AND MATHEMATICS

Motivates Learning

Since children's literature is written about today's children's experiences, about their lived world and reflects their emotions, as well as covers topics of relevance to them in a meaningful context (Hancock, 2008; Lynch-Brown & Tomlinson, 2008), it appeals and engages them and motivates learning.

In this regard, "when numbers and their operations are embedded in meaningful real-world contexts children are able to make sense of the mathematics, gain mathematical power and develop a wider view of the place of mathematics in their world" (Hunsader, 2004, p. 619). "Tying mathematics to stories humanizes the activity and also gives purpose and meaning to mathematics for . . . children" (Griffiths & Clyne, 1988, p. 5), as well as assists in breaking down the artificial dichotomy that sometimes exists between *learning* mathematics and *living* mathematics (Whitin & Wilde, 1992, pp. 2–5).

Investigation Connection

Quack and Count (Baker, 2004) Investigation—The number 7 is presented skillfully and meaningfully as the sum of two addends as seven frolicking ducklings take a swim in a nearby pond. The text, "7 ducklings, 1 plus 6/In the water playing tricks," presents the concept of addition in an unobtrusive way.

Develops and Stretches the Imagination

Children's literature helps children consider ideas and experiences in different ways (Kiefer, Hepler, & Hickman, 2007). It "invites the imagination . . . [It] becomes a way to look beyond things as they are . . . . It permits [children] to create new combinations, alternatives and possibilities . . . . It becomes an essential part of how [children] reason and understand" (Langer, 1995, p. 8).

Investigation Connection

One Big Building: A Counting Book About Construction (Dahl, 2005) Investigation—Children who dream of exploring a construction site, climbing a scaffold to the tenth floor, or getting behind the wheel of a big truck or crane will be better motivated to deepen their understanding of cardinal number or explore multiple representations of a number when learning tasks are based on this text and illustrations.

Fosters Communication

One of the standards of mathematics (National Council of Teachers of Mathematics [NCTM], 2000) and standards for language arts (National Council of Teachers of English [NCTE] & International Reading Association [IRA], 1996) focuses on the importance of communication to promote mathematical thinking and reasoning. Both state the significance of communicating effectively through spoken, written, and visual language/representation to a variety of audiences and for various purposes. The following is stated in *Principles and Standards for School Mathematics* (NCTM, 2000):

> [Communication] is a way of sharing ideas and clarifying understanding. Through communication, ideas become objects of reflection, refinement, discussion, and amendment. [It] helps build meaning and permanence for ideas and makes them public. When [children] are challenged to think and reason about mathematics and to communicate the results of their thinking to others, orally or in writing and others ways of representing, they learn to be clear and convincing. (p. 60)

Children's books, which depict explicit or implicit mathematical understandings in a nonthreatening tone and in context of the children's lived world, have the potential to engage children in meaningful and reflective conversations, discussions, and investigations in productive mathematics discourse. They provide the children a natural way to use and connect book language to their own lives, to reflect on their thoughts, and to generate new thoughts and new ways of thinking. Griffiths and Clyne (1988) assert that communication of this nature helps children to develop their mathematical understandings.

Investigation Connection

One Is a Snail, Ten Is a Crab: A Counting by Feet Book (Sayre & Sayre, 2010) Investigation—Children are asked, "Why do the authors say 'that 30 is three crabs'?" Following adequate time to think about the question—try different strategies—they share their reasons and explain and justify them. Such experience provides the children the opportunity to learn to clarify their thinking and reasoning and how to present such in a convincing manner to their peers.

For the children's communication in mathematics to be relevant and understood by their peers and others, they need to have opportunities to be exposed to and explore the language of mathematics. As Whitin and Whitin (2000) state, "Math is language too." They need to have opportunities to connect the abstract language of mathematics to their everyday lives (Whitin & Whitin, 1996) and "grapple with mathematical concepts in a meaningful context" (Griffiths & Clyne, 1988, p. 3).

Investigation Connection

Minnie's Diner: A Multiplying Menu (Dodds, 2007) Investigation—In this hilarious story, children encounter such mathematical terms as *twice* and *double* and explore their meanings through text and illustrations—for example, "[Phil] raced to the diner. He burst through the door, **twice as big** as his brother before. 'I'll have what Bill has, but make it a double.'"

Writing and other ways of representing, such as drawings, modeling, pictures, using objects, symbols, and drama, are also valuable means to communicate. They, too, are ways by which children can "articulate, clarify, organize, and consolidate their thinking" (NCTM, 2000, p. 128). In regard to young children's writing, Whitin and Whitin (2000) state that it plays an important part in their language growth and is "a tool for discovery in mathematics" (p. 3). It provides the children opportunities to make sense of how print communicates a message, to develop an understanding of the features of clear communication, and to reflect. When writing, they call on and use their book knowledge and book features, such as words, phrases, and textual structure (Kiefer et al., 2007).

Investigation Connection

How Many Snails? A Counting Book (Giganti, 1994) Investigation—Children choose an object of interest and create a double-page spread similar to one in the book.

The more children communicate their mathematical thinking and reasoning through writing and other ways of representing, the more they learn to use more precise mathematical language and the more they learn to use conventional symbols to express their mathematical ideas. "Communication makes mathematical thinking observable and therefore facilitates further development of that thought" (NCTM, 2000, p. 128). In addition, it "helps to build a collaborative community (of learners) that enables children to generate ideas, develop a personal voice, and reflect upon their current (mathematical) understandings" (Whitin & Whitin, 2000, p. 6).

Fosters Critical and Creative Thinking and Problem Solving in a Natural Way

Making observations, predictions, inferences, comparisons, evaluations, and summaries requires children to reflect on their thinking and reasoning. These are built-in features of any meaningful book discussion and subsequent Investigations, as well these features are the essence of meaningful mathematical inquiry (Freeman & Goetz Person, 1998; Kiefer et al., 2007; Morrow & Gambrell, 2004; Schiro, 1997). As children search for responses and justification of them, they have to explore prior mathematical knowledge and reflect on thinking and reflective skills.

Investigation Connection

Two Ways to Count to Ten (Dee, 1988) Investigation—Children are challenged along with King Leopard's fellow beasts to think about the different ways to count to ten and to determine which way is the quickest and cleverest. They are required to use their critical and problem solving skills to determine the solution.

Enriches All Areas of the Curriculum

Children's lived world "is not fragmented into disciplines, and disciplines are not fragmented into facts and subskills" (Stice, Bertrand, & Bertrand, 1995, p. 406). Their lived world is not "compartmentalize into math, science and social studies" but rather, they apply "the content, skills and processes (they) have learned to think about, discuss and solve real-life problems and situations" (Freeman & Goetz Person, 1998, p. 19). This is applicable in any educational setting. Children's learning and curriculum are more than the sum of their parts; they are integrated. When they engage in authentic mathematical experiences, through children's books, they draw on and integrate content, processes, and skills from other curriculum areas. The books connect content and strategies in a meaningful and natural way, challenge the intellect, help make sense of the world, inspire inquiry, support and extend understandings and concepts, and provide depth and richness of detail to any mathematical understanding or topic within and across the entire curriculum (Hancock, 2008; Kiefer et al., 2007; Whitin & Whitin, 2004).

Investigation Connection

The Water Hole (Base, 2004) Investigation—Children may enhance their understanding of numbers one through ten, as well as study wildlife from different countries and "in the process giving the central image of the water hole a certain metaphorical significance" through an in-depth study of this book. Such a study provides the children the opportunity to explore the book's mathematical and literary features and focuses on learning expectations from the social studies, science, and art curricula at the same time, consolidating their thinking and learning.

All children's literature selected for this book to introduce and support the mathematical understandings to be explored and learned throughout the Investigations reflect several, if not all, of these important reasons for integrating children's literature and mathematics. According to Whitin and Wilde (1992), integrating children's books and mathematics helps children to see how mathematics is relevant to their daily lives and helps them to develop a broader view and an appreciation of mathematics in their lived world.

SUMMARY

Children's literature provides a meaningful lived world context for young children to be introduced to, explore, and learn mathematical understandings. Quality mathematics related books embed numbers and their operations in authentic settings that enable the children to make sense of mathematics, gain mathematical power, and develop a wider view of the significant of mathematics in their lives.

Essential Features of the Investigations 4

DESIGN OF INVESTIGATIONS

In this book, it is the learning experiences, mainly referred to as problem solving tasks, outlined in the Investigations that will have the most impact on children's learning. The design of the Investigations integrates the following features into the learning experiences:

- The Context
- Important Mathematics
- Supporting Children's Learning

THE CONTEXT

The mathematics that young children learn in their early years of schooling must incorporate contexts as experienced in their lived world. As Donaldson (1978) argues, young children learn in contextualized situations, concepts that they fail to learn out of context. During these early schooling years, children need repeated contact with important mathematical ideas in varying contexts at different times throughout the year and from year to year (Small et al., 2004). One learning resource for mathematics that provides these opportunities is children's literature. It presents contexts that children can readily relate to; allows for use of everyday language that can easily be connected to the more formal language and symbolism of mathematics; and is valuable for deepening, reinforcing, and making connections to new knowledge learnt in a different setting. As stated by Perry and Dockett (2000), "Literature can provide a very useful link between something which most children seem to enjoy and mathematics" (p. 83).

Investigation Connection

Olly and Me 1 • 2 • 3 (Hughes, 2009) Investigation—In this realistic picture story-book, number is woven meaningfully into the daily experiences of two young children, Katie and her little brother, Olly. Whether they are playing with their friends, going to the beach, riding on the bus, or being at home, Katie and Olly always find things to count, building their familiarity with numbers. This gentle story portrays effectively how learning numbers from 1 to 10 can be fun and how significant numbers are in children's lives.

"Mathematically proficient [children] can apply the mathematics they know to solve problems arising in everyday life, society, and the workplace. In early grades, this might be as simple as writing an addition equation to describe a situation" (Common Core State Standards Initiative [CCSSI], 2012a, p. 2). There are many tasks throughout the Investigations that ask children to write equations to represent a lived world situation.

Investigation Connection

Centipede's 100 Shoes (Ross, 2003) Investigation—Children write an equation to help find the solution to the following word problem: "Crawley, the centipede, hides some shoes under the log. She gives 32 to her friend. Now she has 27 shoes. How many shoes did Crawley hide?"

IMPORTANT MATHEMATICS

The problem solving tasks that comprise the Investigations explore a wide variety and balance of mathematical concepts, procedures, and processes that engage children in mathematical reasoning and problem solving. They focus on the mathematics set down in the standards for mathematical content (CCSSI, 2012a), interwoven with the standards of practice (CCSSI, 2012a), and in keeping with the following statement: "Mathematical understanding and procedural skills are equally important, and both are assessable using mathematical tasks of sufficient richness" (CCSSI, 2012a, p. 4).

It is the intention of the authors that these tasks involve children in important mathematics that is "sound and significant" (National Council of Teachers of Mathematics [NCTM], 2007) and "rich in content and processes" (NCTM, 2007), and always with an eye on the learning expectations stated for the Investigation. The following sections elaborate on the mathematical content and processes included in each Investigation.

Content

The mathematical content of the problem solving tasks throughout the Investigations is based on the learning expectations associated commonly with developing number sense for young children. The learning experiences provided for the children to meet these expectations integrate, where appropriate, with other strands of the mathematics curriculum and the processes of mathematics and language arts.

A crucial aspect of learning important mathematics is learning to communicate this mathematics. It is through communication—that is, oral, written, and other ways of representing—that children learn to effectively share their mathematical thinking and reasoning and clarify their understanding with their peers and others. In this regard, standards from the *Common Core State Standards for English Language Arts* (CCSSI, 2012a) are included in the learning expectations for each Investigation.

Since the release of *The Curriculum and Assessment Standards for School Mathematics* (NCTM, 1989), number sense is considered an essential goal for young children, as it is for all children and adults to live productive lives in society. There may not be agreement on a common definition of number sense, but there is a general consensus that children with number sense have an intuitive knowledge of numbers and the operations and are able to use this knowledge in flexible ways to make mathematical judgments, solve problems, and to perform mental mathematics and estimations. Number sense grows and develops over time. The following key ideas about number are important for this growth and development in the four- to eight-year-old child:

- Sorting and classifying sets
- Recognizing patterns and relationships in our number system
- Counting in different ways
- Subitizing
- Making connections among numbers represented in multiple ways
- Learning about the composition and decomposition of numbers
- Comparing numbers
- Place value
- Adding and subtracting in different ways
- Discovering the properties of addition and subtraction (CCSSI, 2012a; Dacey & Collins, 2010; NCTM, 2006, 2010)

The Investigations actively engage young children in rich problem solving tasks to develop and apply these key ideas, resulting in a deep understanding of number and the operations and using this understanding to deepen their knowledge of mathematics, solve problems, and develop number sense.

Investigation Connection

Quack and Count (Baker, 2004) Investigation—One task asks children to "Find all the ways that 6 can be written as the sum of two numbers," engaging children in exploring an important relationships in mathematics—that is, the decomposition and composition of numbers, referred to by Van de Walle (1998) as "the most important relationship that can be developed about number" (p. 100). At the same time children are also learning and reinforcing basic addition facts to seven, easily extended to include basic facts to eighteen. While exploring this task, children may wonder if $2 + 4$ is the same as $4 + 2$ and, if so, how are they the same? It is a time when the teacher may introduce commutativity, an important property of the addition of numbers. Children's interest and curiosity are sparked further when given the opportunity to generalize about this property by questions such as, "Does this apply to addition of all numbers?"—the beginning of algebraic reasoning. They are also seeing how numbers are used in their lived world.

Process

Children are learning important mathematics when exploring the previously given task, but they are also engaged in modeling, reasoning, representing, communicating, making connections, and problem solving. The cognitively challenging tasks in each Investigation engage children in "doing, talking, reflecting, discussing, observing, investigating, listening, and reasoning" (Copley, 2000), ways in which children primarily make sense of the mathematics they are learning.

Investigation Connection

The Tub People (Conrad, 1995) Investigation—First, children become involved physically with finding all the ways the seven people can be arranged on the side of a tub and on the floating soap, using a storyboard and concrete objects to represent the people. While challenged to represent the arrangements symbolically in charts, orally, and in words, and then making connections among these three forms of representation, they are engaged in important mathematics that young children need to learn.

After finding all possible solutions to the problem, "How many arrangements of 7 people in 2 places?" they are expected to justify to their learning community why they think they have found all the arrangements. They make predictions and generalize when asked in this same Investigation, "If there were 8 Tub People how many ways do you predict they could be arranged? How do you know?" This line of questioning is extended to other numbers of Tub People, until finally the children are asked, "How many ways do you predict they could be arranged if there is any number of Tub People?" Again, this is the beginning of algebraic reasoning for young children.

SUPPORTING CHILDREN'S LEARNING

Young children's learning is greatly impacted by how supportive the environment is in which their learning is nurtured. Adults can enhance the children's learning by "providing environments, rich in language, where thinking is encouraged, uniqueness is valued, and exploration is supported" (NCTM, 2000, p. 74). Throughout the Investigations in this book there are many suggestions made to promote and support a learning environment that ensures children learn important mathematical concepts and procedures and also focuses on children's reasoning, communicating, representing, making connections, and sense making.

Baroody (2000) cautions that learning is more likely to occur if adults mediate children's learning experiences. They need to scaffold children's experiences and provide support or assistance when children are working on a task, so as to enhance and extend children's learning (Vygotsky, 1986). In this book, the learning experiences throughout the Investigations use a child-centered, pedagogical approach in which scaffolding is used consistently to improve children's communication and reflection and, hence, their learning.

Investigation Connection

How Many Snails? A Counting Book (Giganti, 1994) Investigation—Such questions and prompts as "What is the question asking us to find?" or "Why did that happen?" or "Where did you get this?" or "Tell me more about what you are thinking" challenge children to clarify and evaluate their reasoning.

Minnie's Diner: A Multiplying Menu (Dodds, 2007) Investigation—Probing questions, a form of scaffolding—such as, "How did you decide what to do first?" or "Do you think you found all possibilities?" or "How do you know?"—encourage children to reflect on what they or their peers are doing, communicate further their reasoning, and build on their prior knowledge.

Chapter 2, The Learning Environment, gives a more in-depth description of an effective, supportive mathematical learning environment for young children.

SUMMARY

The Investigations are introduced through a children's book and explored through an inquiry problem solving approach where there is a balance between the development of conceptual and procedural knowledge, often all happening simultaneously. Besides developing and consolidating important mathematical content and problem solving strategies, the tasks within each Investigation promote reasoning, engaging in communication, making connections, and designing and analyzing representations. The Investigations reflect a child-centered, pedagogical approach in which scaffolding is used consistently to improve children's communication, reasoning and reflection, and, hence, their learning.

5 Design of the Investigations

STAGES OF THE INVESTIGATIONS

The Investigations are designed so that children are actively involved in rich problem solving tasks, organized into six stages—namely, read aloud, engage, explore, consolidate, extend, and reflection and discussion. At each stage children are encouraged and challenged to use their own strategies and prior knowledge to find solutions to problems posed in the tasks and then share these with peers and teacher.

The learning expectations are stated clearly at the beginning of each Investigation. They are selected from the *Common Core State Standards for Mathematics* (Common Core State Standards Initiative [CCSSI], 2012b), *Curriculum Focal Points for Pre-Kindergarten Through Grade 8 Mathematics* (NCTM, 2006), the *Common Core Standards for English Language Arts* (CCSSI, 2012a), *Standards for the English Language Arts* (National Council of Teachers of English [NCTE] & International Reading Association [IRA], 1996), and Canadian Provincial Guidelines for Mathematics and Language Arts.

THE SIX STAGES

Read Aloud

There are many intrinsic and extrinsic reasons why the authors decided to introduce young children to the learning expectations explored in each Investigation through a read aloud of a quality mathematics-related children's book. However, for the purpose of this book, two will be referenced.

The first and foremost reason for the read aloud stage is to provide the children the opportunity to discover personally the delights in the story and to appreciate the story for story sake—that is, its content, language, and power to ignite their imaginations, piquing their curiosity and helping them entertain ideas in new ways without being questioned (Kiefer, Hepler, & Hickman, 2007;

Strong, 1988). In addition, it gives the children the opportunity to connect independently the story's content to their lives. Reading aloud such stories as *Minnie's Diner: A Multiplying Menu* (Dodds, 2007) with its comical storyline; rhythmical pattern; and hilarious, exaggerated illustrations heightens children's joys and engagement in story. As Whitin and Wilde (1992) reiterate, the first read aloud should be to allow the children to "Enjoy the story. Don't destroy the magic of a story by interrupting it with mathematical questions as you read it aloud" (p. 18). Discovering the pleasures enhances children's desire to return to the book again and again. The more they return to the book, the more familiar they become with the story, the more content they comprehend, and the more connections and interrelationships they make between the content and their lived world (Freeman & Goetz Person, 1998).

The second reason for the read aloud stage is to introduce children to, familiarize them with, and build their knowledge about a particular mathematical content and processes—for example, "to add two or more one- and two-digit numbers to get a given number" as noted in *One Is a Snail, Ten Is a Crab: A Counting By Feet Book* (Sayre & Sayre, 2010) Investigation; "to explore the concept of decomposition of number" through *Quack and Count* (Baker, 2004) Investigation; and "to find multiple solutions to a problem" in *The Tub People* (Conrad, 1995) Investigation.

Besides the initial read aloud, research shows that rereading aloud a book to children is as important as the initial read aloud (Kiefer et al., 2007). In fact, with repeated read alouds of the same book, its content becomes more familiar to the children and their responses to it are enhanced and increased in number, variety, and complexity (Morrow & Gambrell, 2004; Pappas, Kiefer, & Levstik, 1999). As well, Booth (1998) maintains that children's responses become "more interpretative and they begin to predict outcomes and make associations, judgments and elaborative comments" (p. 45).

Although the authors of this book do suggest specifically when to reread aloud a book—for example, during the engage stage of an Investigation, the decision is the teacher's and children's to determine where and when, as well as with whom.

Engage

The main purpose of the engage stage is to introduce children to specific learning expectations through problem solving tasks, related directly to the children's book read during the read aloud stage. The tasks are primarily at a concrete level using a variety of manipulatives, commonly associated with number. At this stage, children work with partners or in small groups and are given many opportunities to share strategies and solutions and to support each other. The tasks are of a difficulty level that most children can feel comfortable engaging in and experiencing success. As well, they provide the teacher with an opportunity to assess the children's readiness to explore more deeply the same learning expectation at later stages of the Investigation.

Investigation Connection

Mouse Count (Walsh, 2001) Investigation—Children working in pairs with a concrete model of a mouse read together, "Soon he found four more . . . , fast asleep." The teacher asks, Do you see four mice on the page? and allows time for children to convince each other that there are four mice on the page either by counting the mice in the illustration by touching or matching with the concrete model.

They continue reading, "And he counted them: Four . . . five . . . six . . . seven." The teacher asks, Why does the snake say: "Four . . . five . . . six . . . seven"? The children share responses with partners and the whole group. This is followed by a discussion focusing on why the snake started counting at four. During this time, the teacher observes children who are not ready for the "counting on" strategy and those who are ready to move to the explore stage of the Investigation.

Explore

The focus of the explore stage, in each Investigation, is to assist children to make further relationships and connections to previous knowledge, construct new knowledge, and represent this new knowledge in multiple ways—for example, concretely, pictorially, graphically, symbolically, and in writing. Children are using their representations to scaffold their own reasoning, demonstrate it to others, and make connections to previous knowledge. By looking carefully at children's representations, teachers are provided with a window into children's reasoning.

During this stage children are also expected to share orally their strategies and solutions, listen to the reasoning of others, and justify their own reasoning. The teacher plays an important role at this stage, observing children as they work at finding solutions, asking questions to clarify or further stimulate their thinking, and making decisions about how and which solutions are shared with the whole group. The Investigations in this book provide support to have this happen.

Investigation Connection

The Water Hole (Base, 2004) Investigation—Children explore the learning expectation "to relate a numeral and a number word, 1 to 10, to its respective quantity." During the engage stage of the Investigation, they identified the numeral, number word on each page and counted the corresponding objects. Now, they delve further into the expectation by choosing their favorite number, one to five, and represent it on a 4 x 6 index card. Different representations are encouraged, using ideas from illustrations in the book, such as numeral, number word, drawings of favorite animal, tallies. The numeral is colored and patterned to match their favorite animal, similar to the illustrator's depiction; yarn is attached to the card and hung around each child's neck. The children join hands and, with music playing, dance around in a circle. When music stops the children find a match or matches for the number on their neck. If there is no match, they find the child with the number closest to theirs. Children with like numbers stand together, telling how they know they have a match; how their representations are the same; how they are different; or why they chose a close number. They discuss why some numbers are more popular than others, why some are not chosen, or why a particular number is chosen by only one person.

Consolidate

The purpose of the consolidate stage is to help the children consolidate their learning. The tasks involve children working individually or in small groups to do purposeful and meaningful practice of what they have learned at the previous three stages and to further make sense of the learning expectations explored. It is also a time when children are encouraged to generalize solutions.

Investigation Connection

The Water Hole (Base, 2004) Investigation—There are four tasks suggested to help children consolidate their learning. One of these asks that each child be assigned a number from one to ten, find the corresponding page to the assigned number in the book, and then do the following:

- Print the numeral on the top of a blank page.
- Draw and illustrate favorite animal showing color and skin texture.
- Illustrate numeral similar to the illustrator's style.
- Print the number word, the animal's name, and a brief description.

The pages are collated to create a number book 1 to 10.

Extend

The extend stage has optional tasks for children, challenging them to extend their learning of mathematical content—and sometimes different from the main learning expectations explored in the four previous stages. Often, the provided tasks have children connect to real-life situations or to other parts of the curriculum—for example, art, science, and social studies.

Investigation Connection

How Do You Count a Dozen Ducklings? (Chae, 2006) Investigation—Mama Duck counts the twelve ducklings and says, "That's a lot of ducklings." What do you think she means? Do you think it is a lot of ducklings? Why or why not?

Reflection and Discussion

Jerome Bruner (1960), educational theorist, maintains that central to all learning is reflection. It is a process of "turning ideas over in your head, thinking about things from different points of view, stepping back to look at things again, consciously thinking about what you are doing and why you are doing it" (Hiebert et al., 1997, p. 5). Reflection and communication are integrated processes, and in this regard, Dosemagen (2007) says, "Reflection alone is yet another internal mental act. Combined with communication, however, reflection becomes an important indicator of what is and is not understood" (p. 155).

Included at the end of each Investigation there is a section titled Reflection and Discussion. It provides questions and prompts to guide both children and teachers as they think consciously about and communicate their experiences and feelings they had while engaged in the Investigation. As reflections are shared with peers and colleagues in person, online or using web based technology, learning is enhanced and teaching improved to better meet the needs of all children.

Investigation Connection

Ten Little Fish (Wood, 2004) Investigation—Children (individual or small group) and teacher-posed questions:

- Which do you find easier to do: "counting forward" from 1 to 10 or "counting backwards" from 10 to 1? Why do you think that is?
- What strategies do you have for counting backwards? Do they always work? What do you do if they don't?
- When do you think counting backwards would be useful for you?

The Tub People (Conrad, 1995) Investigation—Teacher(s): If possible, share and discuss responses with colleagues.

- How long do you allow your children to wrestle with finding the solution to a problem (e.g., all the ways to arrange seven people) before you offer help? Do you give hints or ask questions to get them thinking more deeply?
- What challenges do you face in motivating all the children to want to find the solutions to a problem?
- What changes might you make to your instructional strategies so that more children will be motivated to find all solutions to a task?
- Share your children's understanding of 0 as a number?

SUMMARY

The structure of the Investigations, organized into six stages, allows for children to make sense of the mathematics they are learning, and at the same time, it offers support for the teacher to observe and reflect on this learning so instruction can be adjusted to children's needs.

PART II

Children's Literature and Number Sense Investigations

Unit I

Counting and Cardinality

CARDINAL NUMBER ONE TO TEN

The Water Hole

Graeme Base

Summary: A captivating 1 to 10 counting book! However, besides being a counting book, it's a puzzle book and an art book fused ingeniously together by the noted Australian author and illustrator Graeme Base. While exploring the concept of each number, its numeral, number word, and pictorial representation, Base takes one on an exciting, informative journey to the plains of Africa, the forests of India, the deserts of outback Australia, the Galapagos Islands, and beyond, visiting various indigenous animals and their habitats. Each vibrant, rich, detailed illustration of watercolors, pencil, and gouache depicts the plush landscape of each region or country and the animals and their habitats. In addition to the main indigenous animal depicted in the illustration, Base frames each double-page spread with a top and bottom border of 10 other indigenous animal silhouettes and their names from the specific area. These animals are hidden cleverly in the landscape—that is, in the trees, weeds of the main illustration.

INVESTIGATION: GET YOUR HOOF OUT OF MY EAR
Mathematics and Literature Experiences

Learning Expectations:

- To relate a numeral and a number word, 1 to 10, to its respective quantity
- To solve quantitative problems, such as finding the number of objects in a pictorial representation or set and producing sets of a given size

- To represent numbers in multiple ways
- To explore and connect mathematical language in a meaningful way
- To acquire information and build understanding from a nonfiction text
- To create a written text using a familiar literary format

Learning Resources: Multiple copies of *The Water Hole*; multiple sets of numeral, number word, and pictorial cards (1 to 10); linking cubes, string/yarn, and music

Read Aloud (Whole Group, Teacher as Reader):

Note: *Become familiar with the book before reading aloud, noting font sizes, indicating use of various intonations. As well, read* The Water Hole *without any planned stops, unless a child needs further clarification.*

- Explore the book jacket. Ask the following questions:
  - What do you think this book is about? Why?
  - Point to the title, read it, and ask the following question: Why do you think the author called the book *The Water Hole*?
  - Point to the author's name, read it, and ask the following question:
    - Who illustrated the book?
    - How do you know?
  - Point to the illustrator's name and read it. Discuss the fact that Graeme Base is the author and illustrator, and talk about the role of each.
  - Discuss the book jacket's illustration and how it is related to the title.
- Read aloud the entire book, providing time for the children to view the illustrations and find the animals noted in the text.
- If a child initiates a discussion related to the book after **Read Aloud** is completed, provide time for it.
- Place multiple copies of the book in a math center for independent, peer, and home reading.

Engage (Teacher, Whole Group):

- Read together the first double-page spread. Ask the following questions:
  - How many rhinos are there? How do you know?

Note: *Some children may point to the rhino, count, and say, "one"; another may say "I just know," pointing to the numeral "1" and say, "It says one"; another may say, "I read one rhino" pointing to the words.*

- Repeat the previous questions for the remaining pages, numbers 2 to 10, making connections between the numeral, number word, and pictorial representation.
- Discuss each double-page spread:
  - Look at the numeral—for example, 1. Ask the following questions:
    - What do you notice about how the numeral is illustrated?
    - What do you notice about the colors and patterns used in depicting the numeral?
    - Why does Graeme Base illustrate the numeral this way?

> **Engage Observations:**
> - What do the children notice about the way the numeral is depicted? What connections do they make to the illustration?
> - Are the children able to connect the different number representations—pictorial, numeral, printed and spoken word?
> - What challenges do they have in counting the animals? Why? What strategies do they use to help them?
> - Are they accurate in their counting?

Explore:

Task A (Partners, Whole Group):

Resources: String and linking cubes

- Using string, make a floor model of the water hole (ends not tied to allow hole to become smaller as numbers get larger, modeling situation in the story).
- Revisit the numeral 2 illustration, and count the tigers. Each child takes that many cubes, joins them, and shows a partner who checks for accuracy.
- One child places his or her cubes (one at a time) into the water hole, and all count as cubes are dropped. Together they say how many cubes are in the hole.
- Continue the activity to the number 10, children taking turns to place cubes in the hole, one by one.
- As cubes are added, a child is chosen to make the hole smaller. Discuss why the hole is shrinking.

Note: *Observe if a child adds one cube to the number of cubes already in the hole (counting on strategy) or if he or she removes all of them and starts counting from one. See the Counting On—Mouse Count (Walsh, 2001)* **Investigation** *for development of "counting on" strategy.*

Task B (Individual, Whole Group):

Resources: Index cards, yarn, and music

- Each child chooses a number, 1 to 5, and represents it on a 4 x 6 index card. Encourage different representations based on illustrations in the book, such as numeral, word, drawings of favorite animal, tallies, and use of color and patterns.
- Children attach yarn to their card and hang it around their neck; then they all join hands. With music playing, the children dance around in a circle. When music stops the children find a match(es) for their number. If there is no match, find the closest number.
- Children with like numbers stand together and tell the following:
  - How they know they have a match
  - How representations are the same

o How they are different
o Why they chose a close number
- Discuss why some numbers are more popular than others, some not chosen, or some chosen by only one person.
- This **Task** may be repeated for the numbers 6 to 10.

Variation:

- Find a partner where either of the following occurs:
  o Both numbers add to a specified sum.
  o Both numbers differ by one or two.

Task C (Individual, Whole Group):

Resources: Numeral, word, and picture cards—1 to 5

- Distribute cards randomly to the children.
- Call a number from 1 to 5, children with that number represented on their card stand.
- Children with the same representation of a number stand together.
- Numbers can be called first in sequence and then randomly.
- Repeat for numbers 6 to 10.

Explore Observations:
- Are children accurate in counting the pictures of animals to correspond with the number word or numeral and correct number of cubes?
- How do children keep track when they are drawing pictures to represent their chosen number?
- What representations do they use for their number?
- How do they choose a color and pattern to depict their numeral? Does it match the chosen animal?
- What strategies do they use in finding a match for their number?
- When the number named is said orally, can they match it to the symbol, word, and picture cards? Do they recognize at a glance or do they have to use other strategies?
- Do the children use a counting on strategy or always start counting from 1?

Consolidate:

Task A (Individual, Partners, Whole Group):

- Each child completes the **Matching Numeral, Word, and Animal** sheet (Appendix A [1]).
- When the sheet is completed, partners share and check each other's work.
- Sheet can be extended to include numbers to 10.

Task B (Individual, Partners):

Resources: 5-Frame (Appendix A [2]) and counters

Note: *If children have no previous experience with **5-Frames,** demonstrate use on the overhead or whiteboard.*

- Give each child the **5-Frame** and set of counters.

- Call a number—for example, 3. Children use their counters to show it on their **5-Frame.** Partners check each other's work.
- Ask the following question:
    o How do you know you have shown 3?
- Repeat for other numbers 1 to 5, selected randomly.
- Repeat activity for numbers 1 to 10 using the **10-Frame** (Appendix E [1]).

Task C (Individual):

- Assign a number 1 to 10 to each child, and each finds the corresponding double-page spread in *The Water Hole.*
- Each child does the following:
    o Prints the numeral on the top of a blank page
    o Illustrates that number of their favorite animal showing color and skin texture
    o Illustrates numeral similar to the illustrator's style
    o Prints the number word, the animal's name, and a brief description
- Combine pages to make a 1 to 10 counting book. Several counting books may be created. Include a title, author(s) and illustrator(s) names, and dedication for each book.

Consolidate Observations:

- Are children fluent in representing numbers in different ways?
- Are they accurate when counting or drawing objects to match a given number?
- What strategies do they use to design their counting book? Do they give up after making one representation?
- When using the **5-** and **10-Frames,** do they add counters to a given number (or take away) or do they start over to make a given number? Do they work left to right?

Extend:

Task A (Whole Group):

- In *The Water Hole*, read together, "But something was happening" (numeral 3 illustration).

- Ask the following question:
  - ○ What is happening? Why? Discuss.
- Read together, "The pool was getting smaller." Discuss.
- Continue reading together, noting the shrinking water hole.
- Ask the following questions:
  - ○ Why do you think this is happening?
  - ○ Why do animals need water?
  - ○ As water disappears, how do you think the animals are feeling?
- Read together and discuss, "There was nothing to say. The water was all gone." (Numeral 10 illustration).
- Ask the following questions:
  - ○ What do you think the animals will do?
  - ○ How might they get water?
  - ○ Who else needs water besides animals?
- Read together and discuss, "And all the animals went away."
- Ask the following questions:
  - ○ Where do you think the animals went?
  - ○ Do you predict that they will come back? Why?
- Children may do a follow-up project on water conservation; the importance of rain.

Task B (Whole Group):

- Find and count the frogs on each page.
- Ask the following question:
  - ○ What do you notice?

Note: *This could lead to a discussion of why the illustrator shows a fewer number of frogs as the water hole shrinks or how frogs are considered as an indicator of a declining environment. Frogs are considered as nature's canary in the mine. Discuss.*

Task C (Small and Whole Groups):

Resources: Stickers and world map or globe

- List, on overhead or whiteboard, the countries cited in *The Water Hole.*
- Each small group selects a country, finds it on the map or globe, and places a sticker on the country. On each sticker write the name of the animal illustrated for that country.

Task D (Whole or Small Groups):

- Retell *The Water Hole* from the frogs' point of view. Using shared writing technique, write the retelling. Make a big book.

Task E (Small and Whole Groups):

- Children are assigned different double-page spreads. On paper, they find and record the number of indigenous animals hidden in the top and bottom borders and their names.
- Share findings.

Reflection and Discussion:

Children (Individual, Whole Group, Teacher-Posed Questions):

- Would you recommend *The Water Hole* to friends? If so, to whom and why? If not, why not?
- Was counting the animals illustrated in the book challenging? If so, in what way?
- Do you find it easier to count pictures or cubes? Why?
- What language in the book did you find most interesting? Why?
- Children pose questions and comments.

Teacher(s) (If possible, share responses with colleagues.):

- What did you learn about the children's ability to count and produce numbers to 10?
- "Representations make mathematical ideas more concrete and available for reflection" (National Council of Teachers of Mathematics [NCTM], 2000, p. 137). **Explore** and **Consolidate Tasks** asked children to make multiple representations of numbers. How does the quote apply to your children's learning of number?
- Would you consider engaging your children in an author–illustrator study of Graeme Base? If so, plan your study.
- What changes would you make to the **Investigation** if you were to do it again?
- Teacher's may pose questions and comments.

SUBITIZING

Olly and Me 1•2•3

Shirley Hughes

Summary: A delightful, realistic number book (1–10) portraying the child-centered world of Katie and her little brother Olly. With warmth and gentleness, Hughes weaves meaningfully and effectively number and counting into their daily lived experiences, showing how significant number and counting are in children's lives. Whether they are playing with their friends, going to the beach, riding on the bus, or just being at home, Katie and Olly always find things to count, building their knowledge and understanding of numbers. Besides the text being relevant and appealing, so, too, are the detailed, realistic gouache and oil pastel illustrations, evoking emotions and familiarity. Hughes presents each number with a numeral, a number word, and quantity through pictorial and graphic representations.

INVESTIGATION: QUICK IMAGES TO 5

Mathematics and Literature Experiences

Learning Expectations:

- To recognize quantities up to 10 by subitizing
- To communicate strategies and skills used to recognize a quantity
- To develop spatial visualization skills
- To relate illustrations to the story as it unfolds

Learning Resources: Multiple copies of *Olly and Me 1•2•3*, blank cards (same size as standard numeral cards), dot-faced number cubes (overhead, whiteboard, or game-board size), and circular counters

Read Aloud (Whole Group, Teacher as Reader):

- Explore and discuss the title, book jacket illustration, and pages and their connection to the story.
- Read the author/illustrator's name. Ask: What does an author do? What does an illustrator do?
- Read the entire book, allowing time for the children to view the illustrations.
- At the end of **Read Aloud,** if a discussion is initiated by the children and related to the book, take time for it.
- Place multiple copies of *Olly and Me 1•2•3* in the math center for independent, peer, and home reading.

Engage:

Task A (Whole Group):

- Clap your hands 3 times by doing 2 claps in rapid succession and then 1.
- Ask the following questions:
  o How many claps?
  o How do you know?

Note: *Some children may say, "I counted 1, 2, 3." Others may say, "I heard 2, then 1, and I knew it was 3." It is important for children to hear others explain how they know how many. It makes children's reasoning known to the whole group and other children rethink their reasoning.*

- Clap once, then twice, and then repeat the previously given questions. Gradually increase the number of claps to 5—for example, 3 claps and 2 claps, 4 claps and 1 clap, or 1 clap and 4 claps.
- Repeat different configuration of claps with a variety of sounds.

Task B (Whole Group):

- Jump twice, then once.
- Ask the following questions:
  - ○ How many jumps?
  - ○ How do you know? (See the previous note.)
- Repeat, using other configurations of numbers up to 5.

Task C (Whole Group):

- Roll a large number cube on a table, floor, or overhead.
- Ask the following questions:
  - ○ How many dots do you see on the face?
  - ○ How do you know?
- Continue to roll the cube. Ask questions and share reasoning as previously noted.

Note: *Tasks A–C can be repeated many times before actually doing Task D more directly related to the book.*

Task D (Whole Group):

- Reread aloud the pages up to the number 5.

Note: *Most 4- and 5-year-olds can recognize at a glance how many dots are represented by 1 and 2 dots, so begin with the pages representing 3.*

- Ask the following questions:
  - ○ How many dots are there?
  - ○ How do you know?
- Using circular counters, make the same arrangement. Show it quickly, then cover or take away.
- Ask the following questions:
  - ○ How many counters did you see?
  - ○ How do you know?
- Repeat using a different arrangement of the counters, such as ●● ●
- Ask the following questions:
  - ○ How many do you see?
  - ○ How do you know?
- Repeat for this arrangement: ● ●●
- Repeat for numbers 4 and 5.

Engage Observations:

- What strategies and skills do the children use to tell how many when numbers are arranged in different ways? Do some say I knew there were two and one more is three? Or others just say I knew by looking.

- Do children listen to the strategies used by other children? Do they ever adopt the strategies they hear?
- Do some children continue to want to count the counters and are not able to subitize?

Explore (Individual, Whole Group):

- Model one or two rectangular configurations (nonlinear arrangements) of 3—for example:

(Rectangular cards with punched holes can be used also to show the configurations.)

- Each child makes it with counters and shares how he or she knows it is 3. Answers may vary. Samples are as follows:
  - I just know it is 3.
  - It looks like 3 on the number cube.
  - I saw 1 and 2, and I know that is 3.
  - I saw 1 and 2, and I put them together and got 3.
  - Some may not know and say the following: I need to count them.
- Children make other configurations of 3, 4, and 5 on small rectangular cards (number card size). They then show each one quickly to a partner, cover, and partner tells how many and how they know. Take turns.

Note: *Model the activity with small groups, so children will know how long the card should be shown and the expectation of telling each other how they know.*

Engage Observations:
- Do children find it harder to identify configurations when not arranged linearly?
- What strategies are they using to identify the configurations? Do some just know (perceptual subitizing)? Do others use patterning, grouping of small sets, addition?
- Do they learn from the strategies shared by other children?
- Do some children need to count the dots (or counters) to determine how many?

Consolidate (Individual, Partners, Whole Group):

- Provide children with blank cards (about the size of standard number cards) to record different representations for the numbers 3 to 5. Recordings can be drawn using colored pencils or using stick-on circular dots. They can use their chips to find the arrangements before recording.
- Children place their cards in a stack and take turns quickly showing a card to a partner. One child takes a card from the top of the deck, turns it over, and the other child tells how many he or she saw and how he or she knows.

Consolidate Observations:

- Do the children try to find all the different configurations for the numbers?
- How fluent and accurate are they at identifying the configurations?
- Can they describe orally how they know how many?

Extend:

Task A (Whole Group):

- When children are comfortable in identifying numbers 3 to 5, repeat the **Explore** and **Consolidate Tasks** for numbers 6 to 10, reading the corresponding pages in the book.

Task B (Individual, Whole Group):

- Demonstrate this **Task.** Using the shared writing strategy, select a number and create a double-page spread similar to one in *Olly and Me 1•2•3.*
- Each child chooses favourite number from 1 to 10 and revisits the double-page spread depicting the number in *Olly and Me 1•2•3.* Discuss how the author described in print and represented in illustration the number. Compare to the shared writing double-page spread.
- Each child designs a double-page spread for chosen number.

Reflection and Discussion:

Children (Individual, Whole Group, Teacher-Posed Questions):

- What did you like most about this book? Why?
- What parts of this **Investigation** did you like doing best? Why?

Teacher(s) (If possible, discuss responses with colleagues.):

- What issues or challenges did this **Investigation** raise for your children? Why?
- What issues or challenges did this **Investigation** raise for you? What could be changed to help overcome this issue or challenge?

- What shifts in instructional practice did you make when using this lesson?
- What suggestions do you have to help your children be more successful with subitizing?
- Are children learning from hearing the reasoning of other children?

COUNTING ON

Mouse Count

Ellen Stoll Walsh

Summary: Frolicking in the meadow on a delightful day brings great joy to ten little mice, but while playing, they are always on guard for snakes. One day their playful activities exhaust them, and they become very sleepy. They decide to take a nap, forgetting about the snakes. Unfortunately, a hungry snake finds the sleeping mice and decides to gather them for dinner. Finding a jar, it begins to collect each mouse. While doing so, the greedy snake counts on, "One, two, three . . . Four, five, six, seven . . . " each "little, warm and tasty" mouse. Before the snake has time to eat the mice, one mouse awakens, notices what is happening and tricks the snake by convincing it to gather one more mouse—a big mouse. While slithering over to get the mouse, the mice plan and carry out a successful escape. As they scurry out of the jar, the little mice "uncount" ("ten, nine, eight . . . ") themselves and run home. Walsh's torn paper collage and tempera double-page spreads depict clearly the lively characters of the mice and their escapade, adding to the drama.

INVESTIGATION: COUNTING MICE

Mathematics and Literature Experiences

Learning Expectations:

- To count objects using one-to-one correspondence
- To count forward beginning from a given number within the known sequence (instead of having to begin at 1) and know last number named tells how many
- To find out how many by "counting on" from a given number
- To solve word problems involving the strategy of counting on to find the solution
- To write equations for counting on and addition relationships
- To share and discuss thoughts related to the story
- To ask and respond to questions
- To recognize common types of texts (concept book)

Learning Resources: Multiple copies of *Mouse Count*; mice counters (multi-links, toy stuffed mice, mice puppets made by children, snake puppet or toy), plastic tub, number cubes, plates, linking cubes, **10-Frame** (Appendix E [1]).

Read Aloud (Whole Group, Teacher as Reader):

- Before reading *Mouse Count* to the children, read the story for familiarization, where you may use various intonations, etc.
- Read and discuss the title and the author/illustrator's name, and explore the book jacket's illustration.
- Ask the following questions:
  - What do you think this book is about?
  - Why?
- Read the entire story, without "planned" stops. Give the children time to view each illustration. Enjoy the story for its unfolding drama, and spark the children's interest in counting 1 to 10 and 10 to 1.
- If a discussion, initiated by the children, occurs at the completion of **Read Aloud,** allow time for it.
- Place multiple copies of *Mouse Count* in the math center for independent, partner, and home reading.

Engage:

Task A (Individual, Whole Group):

- One child has a snake puppet or toy; another child is keeper of the jar. The other children each have a "mouse."
- Read together, "It wasn't long before . . . Mouse Count! One . . . two . . . three."
- Ask the following question:
  - How many mice do you see on the page? Share how you counted the mice.

Note: *If some children are having difficulty, suggest placing a counter on each one.*

- The child with the snake puppet chooses three children to drop their mouse one by one into the jar. Children count aloud as mice are dropped by the snake, "One . . . two . . . three."
- Ask the following questions:
  - How many mice are in the jar?
  - How do you know?
- Read together, "Soon he found four more . . . , fast asleep."
- Ask the following question:
  - Do you see four mice on the page? Allow time for children to find the four mice.

Note: *Because the mice in illustrations are somewhat camouflaged it may be difficult for some children to recognize that there are four mice. Suggest using counters to match the mice.*

- Read together, "And he counted them: Four . . . five . . . six . . . seven."
- Ask the following question:
  - Why does the snake say: "Four . . . five . . . six . . . seven." Share responses.

Focus discussion on how many mice are already in the jar and why the snake started counting at four.

Note: *Counting on from 3 to 7 can be problematic and challenging for some children.*

- To confirm there are seven mice in the jar, practice the counting on skill by asking the child with the snake puppet to choose four children to drop their mouse in the jar. Children count on as each mouse is dropped: "four, five, six, seven."
- Ask the following questions:
   o How many mice are in our jar now? How do you know?
   o Did anyone think about it a different way?
- If some children are unsure, take all the mice out and count to confirm there are seven mice in the jar.

Note: *Do not be surprised if some children need to count all the mice starting at one. Not all children are ready to count on. Allow time to take the mice from the jar, and as one child counts the other children double-check the counting.*

- Continue reading together: "At last he found three more . . . fast asleep."
- Ask the following question:
   o Can you see the three mice on the page?
- Allow time to find the three mice.
- Continue reading, "And he counted them: Eight, nine, ten."
- Ask the following questions:
   o Why do you think the snake says, "Eight, nine, ten."
   o How many mice are in the jar?
- Share ideas.
- Continue dramatizing the story, having the snake take the three remaining mice from the children and add them to the jar. As the mice are dropped into the jar the children say together, "Eight, nine, ten."
- Ask the following questions:
   o How many mice are in our jar now?
   o How do you know?
- Allow for different explanations and questions from the children.

Task B (Partners, Whole Group):

Resources: Different colored counters and **10-Frame** (Appendix E [1])

Note: *If children are using **10-Frames** for the first time, take time for them to become familiar with their use.*

- Repeat **Task A**, but this time children model the mice on the **10-Frame.**
- For example: "Mouse Count! One . . . two . . . three." Children start at the top left corner and go left to right.

●	●	●		

- Continue reading, "Soon he found four more . . . , fast asleep."

- Partners place four more mice on their **10-Frame** (use a different color counter).
- Ask the following questions:
  - o What does your frame look like now?
  - o How many mice?
- Count together. Relate to the story.

●	●	●	●	●
●	●			

- Continue reading, "At last he found three more . . . fast asleep."
- Add three more to the **10-Frame.**
- Ask the following question:
  - o How many now?

●	●	●	●	●
●	●	◎	◎	◎

- Retell the story about the mice as shown on their **10-Frame.**
- Partners share and discuss their stories.

Engage Observations:

- How do children count the number of mice on the page? Do they have strategies for keeping track of the sometimes camouflaged mice in the illustrations? Do they model the mice with counters? Does using the counters help?
- How do children count the number of mice dropped in the jar? Do they count on from the number, or do they have to start at 1?
- Do they listen and appear curious about those who use counting on strategies?
- Do they feel confident that counting on will give the correct count?
- When the counting on strategy is shared does it make sense by those who did not do it that way? Do they ask questions to try and understand better?
- Can they connect the language of counting on to finding "how many"?
- Does counting on the numbers, "four, five, six" and "seven, eight, nine" make sense to the children as a way of counting to find how many.
- Are the children able to relate what they did on the **10-Frame** to *Mouse Count?*

Explore:

Task A (Partners, Whole Group):

- Sit in a circle; each set of partners is given ten mice counters and a plate.
- Ask the following question:
  - o On your plate, can you show me three mice?

- One child puts the mice on the plate, and the other double-checks.
- Ask the following questions:
  - Does everyone agree that you have three mice on your plate?
  - Now, on your plate show me four mice.
  - How do you know? How did you get four mice on your plate?
  - Did anyone do it differently?
- Show me five mice. Repeat the questioning that was previously given.
- Show me six mice. Repeat questioning.

Note: *Observe those who take all mice from the plate, and count out the number of mice one by one and those who count on from the mice already on the plate. Allow time for those who count on to share how they did it with others.*

- Remove all mice from the plates.
- Ask the following questions:
  - Can you show me four mice? One child shows the mice, and the partner double-checks.
  - Can you show me six mice? This time observe if children count out two mice and add them to the four, or if they start over from one. Share the different ways the six mice are counted out. Record responses.
- Continue with other numbers up to 8, and ask for a number that is two more each time—for example, show me 6, 8, and 10.
- Repeat with other objects—for example, toy cars, plastic fruit.

Task B (Whole Group):

- Demonstrate this **Task.**
  - I want three mice. Bring me three mice, (child's name), please.
- Put the three mice under a margarine tub (paper cup or slip of paper) where they cannot be seen. (This **Task** may be adapted for the overhead or whiteboard.)
- Ask the following question:
  - How many mice are under the tub? If hesitant, lift the tub and have the child count again. Ask the others if they agree. You could also place the numeral card 3 in front of the tub as a reminder of how many there are.
- Say, "One more mouse comes along." Place the mouse next to the tub.
- Ask the following question:
  - How many mice do we have now? How do you know?
- Together say the following:
  - We have three mice. One more comes along. Now we have four.
- Record the following:
  - The number 3 and one more is 4; write the equation $3 + 1 = 4$.
- Discuss the relationship between the actions, spoken words, and equation.

- Repeat the **Task** with different numbers under the tub that are less than 10, taking the time to do the following:
  - o Determine how many and why.
  - o Write the associated language and addition equation, connecting counting on to addition.

Task C (Whole Group):

- Place two or three objects outside the tub.
- Ask the following questions:
  - o How many mice are there now?
  - o How do you know?
- Continue to record, for example, 5 and 2 more is 7; $5 + 2 = 7$.

Task D (Whole Group):

- Continue **Task C,** but extend to numbers larger than 10.

Explore Observations:

- Do the children add one mouse to the three already counted, or do they start over and count 1, 2, 3, 4?
- Can the children determine the number of mice by saying, "3, 4. There are 4," or do they need to lift the tub and count them all?
- Is it more difficult for the children to count on by two or three than it is to count on by one?
- When they cannot count on, what counting strategies do they use? Are they able to share these strategies with others?
- Are they able to use the mathematical language associated with finding how many when they do it by counting on?
- Are they able to write the associated addition equations?
- Are they associating counting on with adding 1, 2, 3 to a given number?

Consolidate:

Task A (Partners, Whole Group):

Resources: Tub, number cubes, counters, and number cards 1 to 10

- Demonstrate this **Task,** then partners work at a center.
- The first child counts out loud a number of objects and places them under a tub. Place a number card by the tub to tell how many under the tub.
- The second child rolls a number cube with one, two, and three on the faces and places the number of objects as shown on the face of the cube outside the tub.
- The second child tells how many in all and explains why it is so.
- The first child verifies answer and records the corresponding addition equation. Relate to the action that took place.
- Repeat six times by taking turns.

Task B (Partners):

- Find solutions to these story problems.
- Children read together the problem. They can use counters to help find a solution but expect them to represent their solution on paper with drawings and equations.

  A. 3 birds are sitting on the tree.

    1 more flies in and sits next to them.

    How many birds are on the tree now?

  B. Jack puts 5 fish into the tank.

    Jan puts in 2 more.

    How many fish are in the tank now?

  C. Emma bounces the ball 7 times.

    Then she bounces it 3 more times.

    How many times does she bounce the ball?

- After story problems are solved, children write their own story problem, using the same writing format. Children solve each other's problems.
- Give the children two numbers—such as 7 and 3—and ask them to write a word problem using the two numbers and requires addition to find the solution.

Consolidate Observations:

- Can children tell how many objects by counting on, or do they have to count all the objects starting at 1?
- Can they count on when there is only one object to count but find it more problematic when there are two or three objects?
- Do they model the story problems with counters?
- Does modeling help them find a solution?
- Do they need to model all the objects in the problems, or can they say, for example, five birds and then use the counters to count on two more?
- Can they represent on paper how they found their solutions?

Extend:

Task A (Whole Group):

- Read together, "But the snake was very, very hungry, and seven mice were not enough."
- Ask the following question:
  o How many do you think would be "enough"?

Note: *You are not looking for correct answers to "enough" but assessing the children's sense of number and estimation skills. Answers will give a sense of a child's concept of quantity and ability to estimate. Some will remember the number the snake caught from previous reading of the story.*

- Share responses: "How many do they think is enough?"
- Ask the following questions:
  - o Do you think that many mice will fit into the jar?
  - o Why do you think that?

Task B (Partners):

- Solve the following word problems.

Note: *In this set of problems the total number of mice is always 10, and you have to find the number in the jar or the number outside the jar. Children can use counters, drawings, or **10-Frames** to find the solution. They then write an equation to show how the answer was found.*

A. The jar holds 10 mice.

Sylvia, the snake, catches 8 mice and drops them in the jar.

How many more mice does Sylvia have to catch to fill the jar?

B. The jar holds 10 mice.

5 mice are in the jar.

How many mice does Sylvia, the snake, have to catch to fill the jar?

C. The jar has 10 mice.

4 mice crawl out.

How many are still in the jar?

D. The snake fills the jar with 10 mice.

5 mice crawl out.

The snake catches 2 mice and puts them back in the jar.

How many are in the jar now?

- Repeat the problems using different combinations of numbers that have 10 as the sum.

Note: *For the previously given problems all children may not write the equation the same way. It is important to share and compare the different types.*

- For example, for the first word problem one child may write the following:

$8 + \square = 10$

Another may write this:

$10 - 8 = \square$

- Take time to discuss and relate to the strategy used to find the solution.

Task C (Whole Group, Teacher):

- Plan an author/illustrator study of Ellen Stoll Walsh's work:
  - o Discuss what you would like to know about Ellen Stoll Walsh—for example, something about her life, books' themes, what type of books she writes. Make a web of your topics or ideas.
  - o Locate and read her books.

    o Give a book talk for each.
    o Choose topics or ideas from your web, and search for information related to each. Record and share information.
    o Make a book display.
    o Create a concept book and place in your book display.

Reflection and Discussion:

Children (Individual, Whole Group, Teacher-Posed Questions):

- Was *Mouse Count* an appropriate title for this book? Why or why not?
- Are there other titles you would suggest? Share titles and say why they are appropriate.
- What did you like best about doing this **Investigation?**
- What strategies do you have for counting on?
- Why is counting on useful?
- What did you find challenging when writing the equations?

Teacher (If possible, share and discuss responses with colleagues.):

- What ways do you encourage children to listen to one another's sharing of ideas?
- Are they able to follow as another child's explains his or her reasoning?
- Do you consider counting on a more complex counting strategy for some children? Why?
- What ideas do you have to help children become more comfortable with counting on?
- Why do you think it is beneficial to learn to count on?

COUNTING TO FIND HOW MANY

How Many Snails? A Counting Book

Paul Giganti Jr.

Illustrated by Donald Crews

Summary: An intriguing book to ponder and deliberate deeply and to tax one's visual discrimination skills in order to determine "how many in a set and part of a set." Throughout *How Many Snails? A Counting Book*, Giganti asks increasingly more challenging "How many . . . " questions about common things in nature—for example, clouds, flowers, snails; the numbers of books in a library, cupcakes in a bakery, and dogs in the park. Written in a repetitive questioning format, Giganti poses three "how many" questions for each familiar object. Such questions compel one to look carefully at each of Donald Crews's bold, bright gouache double-page spreads to find the answers.

INVESTIGATION A—I WONDER HOW MANY?

Mathematics and Literature Experiences

Learning Expectations:

- To determine how many are in a set and part of a set
- To represent numbers in different ways and make connections among the different representations

- To use spoken and written language to communicate mathematical reasoning coherently and effectively to others
- To recognize language patterns
- To develop concepts about print and an awareness of book language

Learning Resources: Multiple copies of *How Many Snails? A Counting Book*, counters, and chart paper, whiteboard, or overhead

Read Aloud (Whole Group, Teacher as Reader):

- Introduce *How Many Snails? A Counting Book* through its title, author, and illustrator; note and discuss its end pages, title page, and dedication.
- Read for enjoyment the entire story, giving the children time to discover its delight and wonder.
- After **Read Aloud,** place multiple copies of *How Many Snails? A Counting Book* in the math center for independent, peer, and home reading.

Engage (Whole Group):

- Revisit the first double-page spread depicting clouds, and read together each question.
- Invite children to answer. Record responses.
- Follow with questions such as the following:
    - How did you find your answer?
    - Did anyone do it a different way? Did you get the same answer?
    - Did anyone use counters? How did that help?
    - At a glance, how many big and fluffy clouds are there?
    - How did you do that? Tell us more.
    - Did anyone see it a different way?

Engage Observations:

- What strategies do the children use to count objects?
- How do they make use of the illustrations to find answers?
- Are they able to tell how many at a glance (subitize)?

Explore (Small Groups, Whole Group):

- Each group has a copy of *How Many Snails? A Counting Book*. Revisit the illustration of the snails.
- Give the following directions:
    - Represent on paper their solutions of each question. Encourage use of drawings and printing of numerals.
    - Share and check each other's solutions.
    - Share the different strategies used to find solutions.
- Choose groups that used different strategies to share their solutions.

Explore Observations:

- Can children sort the objects they have to count? How do they do that?
- Do they know the last number named tells how many in the set?
- Can they count accurately? Do they double-check? How?
- How do they make use of the illustrations to find answers?
- How do they represent their answers? Do they use numerals?
- Are they able to explain to the group the strategies they used?
- Do children ask questions about each other's strategies?

Consolidate:

Task A (Individual, Small Groups):

- Repeat the **Explore Task** for illustrations depicting flowers, fish, dogs, books, cupcakes, and stars. Since the number and variety of arrangements vary, children may be assigned different illustrations according to needs. Children with the same page can share solutions.

Task B (Individual, Whole, and Small Groups):

- Revisit the first three double-page spreads and read together.
- Ask the following question:
  o What do you notice about the words on these pages? Complete the **Language Pattern Chart** (Appendix A [3]).
- Each child or small group chooses a different object of interest and creates a double-page spread, using the repetitive language structure as in *How Many Snails? A Counting Book*.
- After completion, exchange pages and answer each individual's or group's questions.
- Combine the double-page spreads to make one or more "How many . . . " book(s). Give each book a title. Include author(s)/illustrator(s) names(s). Place the books in the math center for independent or shared reading.

Note: *Have available multiple copies of* How Many Snails? A Counting Book *and the completed* **Language Pattern Chart** *for use by children who may want them for reference.*

Consolidate Observations:

- What strategies are used to complete each section of the **Language Pattern Chart**?
- How do they determine an appropriate title for the completed book(s)?
- What strategies do children use when designing their own page?
- How do they keep track of the number of objects to draw?
- Do they need support to use a language structure similar to that used in the story?
- Do they make sure their questions can be answered from their illustrations?

Extend:

Task A (Individual, Whole Group):

- Discuss and answer the questions posed on the double-page spread of the stars. Share ideas about "very large numbers" and how people might count stars in the night sky.
- Read a book about stars, such as *Stargazers* (Gibbons, 1992) or *Stars* (Simon, 2006). Record the large numbers mentioned.
- Find other books about stars. Share and display them.

Task B (Individual, Whole Group):

- Ask the following questions:
  o What did you notice about the answers to the three questions on each double-page spread of the book? (Numbers get smaller.)
  o Why do you think that is so?

Reflection and Discussion:

Children (Individual, Whole Group, Teacher-Posed Questions):

- When you were answering the author's questions, which ones did you find most challenging? Why?
- When you were making your own page . . .
  o How did you decide on how many objects to draw?
  o How did you keep track of how many to draw in each set?
  o How did you decide what questions to ask?
  o Did your partner have problems answering your questions? Why or why not?
- What did you find most enjoyable about doing this **Investigation**?

Teacher(s) (If possible, discuss your responses with colleagues.):

- What did you learn about your children's reasoning?
- What changes would you make to this **Investigation,** if and when you used it again? Why would you make these changes?
- If need be, what ideas do you have to encourage your children to communicate better with each other and the group?
- How did you decide which children would share their work? Why is this important?
- Why is it important to note if children reread a book?

COUNTING BACKWARDS

Ten Little Fish

Audrey Wood

Illustrated by Bruce Wood

Summary: The mother and son team of Audrey and Bruce Wood have created a "counting backwards" number book featuring a school of 10 multicolored, expressive tropical fish playing gleefully in their turquoise, clear water environment. As they swim around leisurely one fish disappears in each digitally generated double-page spread, leaving one less fish to count. Written in rhyming couplets, with the final number word appearing on the next illustration (e.g., "Six Little Fish, swimming to survive. One likes to hide, and now there are . . . ") creates a predictable text that is engaging and enjoyable.

INVESTIGATION: WHERE DID THEY GO?

Mathematics and Literature Experiences

Learning Expectations:

- To say the number sequence backwards by 1s, starting anywhere from 10 to 1, with and without concrete materials
- To solve word problems that relate counting backwards to subtraction
- To model with mathematics
- To apply a range of strategies to comprehend texts
- To read poetic text to build an understanding of the genre and for personal fulfillment

Learning Resources: Multiple copies of *Ten Little Fish*, numeral cards, storyboard, and counters or ten plastic fish

Read Aloud (Whole Group, Teacher as Reader):

- Explore the book jacket's illustration and title.
- Ask the following question:
  - What do you think the book is about? Why? Discuss responses.
- Read the title.
- Ask the following question:
  - What do you think the book is about? Why? Discuss responses. Relate the title to the illustration.

- Read the author's and illustrator's names. Share information about them—for example, mother and son team.
- Read first double-page spread. Allow time for the children to predict the last word in each rhyming couplet.
- After reading, "One Little Fish. What will he do?" allow time for the children to answer the question? Continue to read.
- If anyone initiates a discussion, allow for it.
- After **Read Aloud,** share how the illustrations are created—that is, digitally generated. Discuss this technique. Make reference to the same technique used by Todd Ouren in *One Big Building: A Counting Book About Construction* (Dahl, 2005).
- Place multiple copies of *One Little Fish* in a math center for independent, peer, and home reading.

Engage (Whole Group):

Task A:

- Dramatize the story. Choose 10 children to represent fish swimming. Provide remaining children with copies of the book *Ten Little Fish* to share. Open to the first double-page spread. Read together, "Ten little fish, swimming in a line." Ask the children (who are not fish) to do the following:
  - Count together to check that there are 10 children representing the 10 fish.
  - Present a numeral card to show how many or hold up fingers to show 10.
- Read together, "One dives down . . . " Choose a child from the swimming fish to dive down, and read "And now there are . . . "
- Ask the following questions:
  - How many are there now?
  - How do you know?
- Count the number of fish left as a recheck and to ensure accuracy. Alternately, one child can be selected to count and others count along. Model orally the language of the action: "There were ten fish and one dived down. Now there are nine." Later this will be related to subtraction.
- Some children (not the fish) show, using their fingers, the number of fish after one dives down; others show by holding up corresponding numeral card.
- The remaining fish (9) continue to "pretend swimming." Read together, "Nine little fish, swimming 'round a crate. One goes in, and now there are . . . "
- Repeat questioning as was just done to determine "how many there are" and why are there that many after one fish leaves? Relate language in the story to the actions and the mathematical language.
- Repeat for remaining numbers until one fish is left, as in the story.

Task B:

- Ask children to share times when they may have counted backwards in their lived world. Record responses.

Engage Observations:

- Do the children count the 10 fish accurately?
- Can they match a numeral card to the number of fish?
- As fish leave one by one, can they keep track on their fingers?
- As fish leave one by one, how do they know how many are left? Do they need to count? Is their counting accurate? Do they know the number that comes before another number?
- Can they state in complete sentences how many fish are left?
- Can they relate counting backwards to events in their lives?

Explore:

Task A (Partners, Whole Group):

- Partners make a storyboard and arrange 10 plastic fish (or counters) on a blue ocean storyboard.
- As the story is reread dramatize the actions with their fish, telling how many are left and justifying how they know. Print the numeral or place a numeral card by the storyboard to show how many are left after each action.
- Connect language in the story to the mathematics.
- Show 10 plastic fish (or counters). Count together to determine how many. As one fish is removed, children tell how many are left and how they know.
- Connect the language of "there are ten fish and one dives down, now there are nine" to subtraction.
- Record $10 - 1 = 9$, and say "There are ten fish and one dives down, now there are 9; 10 minus 1 is 9."
- Reread together the story, relating fish and actions to the numbers and symbolism until you reach $2 - 1 = 1$.

Task B (Whole Group):

- Together recite the number names backwards, starting at 10 (or any other number less than 10 according to needs of children). Repeat.
- Together recite numbers backwards with you saying every second number. Say 10, children say 9, you say 8, they say 7, continue to 1. Repeat.

Explore Observations:

- Are the children becoming more proficient in telling how many are left after one fish leaves?
- Do they need to count the remaining fish or do they just know the number?
- Are some children using the language and concept of subtraction to find how many are left—nine minus one so there are eight left?
- Are they more comfortable in telling how many are left for smaller numbers (e.g., 5 or less)?
- Can they relate the subtraction equations to the actions of the fish?
- Can they recite the number names backwards from 10?

Consolidate (Individual, Whole Group):

Task A:

- Say 3, 2, 1, and ask children to repeat. Record numerals, then have the children read the numerals.
- Follow with 6, 5, 4, and ask children to repeat. Record numerals; then have the children read the numerals.
- Repeat again if necessary.
- Ask children (or an individual child) to start at 6 and count backwards.
- Repeat with other starting numbers up to 10 (e.g., 8, 7, 6 or 10, 9, 8).

Task B (Individual, Partners):

- Each child has a set of numeral cards (e.g., 1–5).
- Starting with 5, they arrange the cards in descending order from left to right. Repeat for other cards—for example, 7 to 3 or 10 to 6; partners check each other's work.

Task C (Whole Group):

- Say a number between 2 and 10 (or hold up a numeral card); children in turn say the number that comes before it.

Task D (Individual):

- Print backwards the numbers from 10 to 1.

Task E (Partners):

Resources: Word Problems (Appendix A [4])

Note: *These word problems connect counting backwards to subtraction.*

- Make a copy of each problem for each pair of children. If necessary read each problem to the children, and allow time for them to find a solution.
- Share solutions with whole group. If children have not written equations bring their attention to a subtraction equation that could be used to solve the problem.

Consolidate Observations:

- Are children fluent in counting backwards?
- When counting backwards and forgetting the next number, do they count forward to find the number?
- When asked the number that comes before a given number, what strategies do they use to determine it? (**Note:** *Counting forwards to determine the next number when counting backwards is a good strategy and shows understanding.*)
- Are they able to find solutions to word problems and explain to others how they found the solution.
- Are they able to write a subtraction equation that could be used to solve a word problem?

Extend:

Task A:

- Extend counting backwards activities above to higher numbers—for example, 20. Using counters and a **100s Chart** (Appendix E [2]) may help children visualize the higher numbers as they count backwards.

Task B (Whole Group):

- Reread *Mouse Count* (Walsh, 2001). After reading, "And while he was gone, the mice rocked the jar one way, and another way, until over it went," children join in to count backwards (uncount), "Ten, nine, eight . . . " The same **Task** may be done with *The Big Storm: A Very Soggy Counting Book* (Tafuri, 2009).

Reflection and Discussion:

Children (Individual or Small Group, Teacher-Posed Questions):

- Which do you find easier to do: counting forward from 1 to 10 or counting backwards from 10 to 1? Why?
- What strategies do you have for counting backwards? Do they always work? What do you do if they don't?
- When do you think counting backwards is useful for you?

Teacher(s) (If possible, share and discuss responses with colleagues.):

- Do your children find counting backwards more difficult than counting forward? Why do you think that is so?
- What other instructional strategies do you have to help children count backwards?
- Do children find it more difficult to say the names of the numbers backward than arranging the numbers backwards using the number cards 10 to 1?
- How do you know if children relate counting backwards to subtraction?
- What changes would you make to this **Investigation** if you were to use it again? Why?

Unit II

Whole Number and Operations Relationships

COMPARING QUANTITIES AND NUMBERS

One Big Building: A Counting Book About Construction

Michael Dahl

Illustrated by Todd Ouren

Summary: A number book that follows the construction of a twelve-story building from its *ONE big plan* to its *TWELVE stories*. For each number, Dahl includes its numeral, number word, and pictorial and graphic representation. The text and illustrations invite children to count and compare numbers. Ouren's digitally generated illustrations in bold primary colors enhance and extend the text, especially such language as *pile drivers*, *concrete mixers*, and *metal beams*. An additional engaging feature is the inclusion of a numeral hidden somewhere in each double-page spread.

INVESTIGATION: MORE MEN OR MORE WOMEN
Mathematics and Literature Experiences

Learning Expectations:

- To compare two sets using one-to-one correspondence and describe them, using comparative words such as *more than*, *fewer than*, or *same as*
- To compare a set to a given referent using comparative language
- To solve a given problem (pictures and words) that involves the comparison of two quantities

- To calculate how many more and how many fewer in given sets of objects
- To represent mathematical ideas in multiple ways
- To develop reading strategies, such as predicting, hypothesizing, and synthesizing
- To understand the meaning and use of punctuation marks

Learning Resources: Multiple copies of *One Big Building: A Counting Book About Construction,* counters, linking cubes, and number cards

Read Aloud (Whole Group, Teacher as Reader):

- Read the entire book for pleasure from the book jacket to the end, allowing time to view the illustrations.
- If a discussion evolves after the completion of the **Read Aloud**, take time for it.
- Place multiple copies of *One Big Building: A Counting Book About Construction* in the math center for independent, peer, and home reading.

Engage:

Task A (Whole Group):

- Talk about "more than, fewer than, same as." Record the words and read them together.
- Allow time to share experiences when they use this comparative language. See the following examples:
  o "I have more stickers than my sister."
  o "There are fewer balls at home than in the school."
- Record all suggestions.

Task B (Partners):

- Each has a container of at least twenty linking cubes.
- Show a numeral card (e.g., 5), and also hold up a 5-cube tower made from linking cubes (could show on the overhead or whiteboard).
- Partners make a 5-cube tower and then are asked to make another tower with more cubes (limit to ten cubes).
- Partners show their tower and tell the whole group why it has more. Model the comparative language—for example, "This tower has more cubes than this one. This tower has two more cubes than this one."
- Repeat with more examples, with emphasis on comparing their two towers and the use of comparative language.
- Repeat by showing an 8-cube tower, and ask the children to make a tower that has fewer cubes than the one displayed.
- Ensure time is allowed to do the following:
  o Explain how they know that the set they made has fewer cubes than the one modeled.
  o Use the language of comparing sets using fewer than.
  o Tell how many fewer cubes their tower has than the one modeled, using comparative language.

Note: *Some children may be perplexed that one group made a tower with a different number of cubes than they did but are still correct—for example, if you show a cube with 5 cubes, children could make one that has 6, 7, 8, 9, or 10 cubes. Similarly, this situation will occur when making towers that have a fewer number of cubes than the given one. Having different answers may leave some children wondering but curious.*

Task C (Individual, Partners, Whole Group):

- Choose two numeral cards (1–10), and show to the whole group.
- Ask each child to do the following:
  - Make a tower that has the same number of cubes as the larger number.
  - Show it to a partner; agree or disagree if tower has the same number of cubes as larger number and how they know.
- Repeat making a tower that has the same number of cubes as the smaller number.
- Repeat this **Task** several times.

Engage Observations:

- Can children relate making comparisons among quantities and numbers to their real life experiences?
- Are children able to make a set that has more than the one shown? How do they do it?
- Do children compare towers by lining up one by the other (measuring) or by counting the blocks?
- Do children wonder when someone makes a tower with a different number of cubes than they did, why it is also considered to be "more than"?
- Can children use the comparison language to talk about their towers?
- Are children able to tell which number is larger when they are shown just the numerals and not a concrete representation?

Explore (Individual, Partners, Whole Group):

- Read together pp. 10–11.
- Ask the following question:
  - What do you see?
- Focus on the people taking a break. Discuss the meaning of *break* in the story's context.
- Pose the following problem:
  - Are there more men or more women taking a break? How many more?
- As children work at finding the solution, you could ask questions, such as the following:
  - What is the question you are asked?
  - What do you need to know to find the solution? How can you find that information?
  - Did you try counting the number of men? Number of women?

- Partners represent on paper how they found the solution.
  - Encourage drawings and use of numbers.
  - Encourage a sentence or two describing the comparison—for example, "There are more men than women," "There is one more man than there are women," or "There are 4 men and 3 women."
- Ask the following questions:
  - How did you know whether there are more men or women? Did anyone know in some other way?
  - How do you keep track of how many of each?
  - What did you do to find out how many more?
  - Does using counters help? Did you record the numbers?
- Questions are asked so whole group understands the strategies and the comparative language used.
- Display solutions.

Explore Observations:

- How do children compare the two sets of women and men? Do they count the sets? Do they record what they counted?
- Do any of the children model the sets with concrete objects (cubes)? How do they use the objects to compare the sets?
- Do they use the language of comparison?
- Can they tell how many more one set is than another? How do they do that—for example, one to one correspondence, finding how many in each set and subtracting?

Consolidate:

Task A (Partners, Whole Group):

- Partners design a page with a construction theme using drawings, numbers, and words that illustrates more women than men.
- Ask the following questions:
  - How do you decide on how many women and how many men to use?
  - How do you keep track of the number of women and men?
  - How are you going to describe your drawing?
  - What sentence are you writing to tell that there are more women than men?
  - How many more women are there? Show us how you know.
- Repeat the **Task,** designing a page that has fewer trucks than cranes.
- In both cases, share the pages with the whole group, explaining what they did and why there are more (fewer) women than men in the illustration. Ask questions to encourage comparative language—for example, how many more or fewer; how they know from their illustration.

Task B (Partners, Whole Group):

Grab the Cubes

- Each partner has a jar with two colors of cubes. Each grabs two handfuls of cubes, sorts the cubes according to color, and makes two towers.
- Ask the following questions:
  o Who has the greater number of cubes of each color?
  o How do you know? Allow time to share answers with each other and also with the whole group.
- Draw each tower, and write the corresponding numerals. Write a sentence comparing the two towers, telling how many more cubes one has than the other.

Task C (Partners):

A Game of Capture

- Partners have a stack of numeral cards (1–10) divided between them. They turn over the top card on their stack, the one with the larger number says, "capture," winning the two cards. When all cards are turned over, each child counts his/her cards and compares totals. One with larger total is the winner. Repeat the game, but this time the one with the smaller number takes the cards.

Task D (Whole Group):

Construction Site Storyboard

- Display an example of a construction storyboard. Arrange two different sets of objects—for example, toy trucks, counters, people. Tell a construction story about the objects to include number of each type of object; which set is more, fewer, or same; and how many more or fewer.
- Change the number and type of objects on the storyboard. Select children to tell a story about the objects using comparative language.
- Partners design a construction storyboard. Encourage use of *One Big Building: A Counting Book About Construction* for ideas. Children place two sets of objects on the board and write comparative sentences describing relation between the two sets of objects.

Consolidate Observations:

- How do children keep track of the numbers when they are designing their own page?
- Are they able to write sentences to describe their drawings?
- Do children work cooperatively when playing **Grab the Cubes** and **A Game of Capture**?
- How do they count the two sets of cubes? Do they double-check?

- How do they compare their cubes? Do they place the towers next to each other and compare them directly? Do they count the number of cubes in each tower and then decide which has more and which has fewer?
- Are they able to represent their findings on paper? Does their representation clearly show the comparisons? Do they use numbers along with drawings?
- When playing **A Game of Capture,** do any of the children make mistakes reading the numerals on the card—for example, mistake 6 for 9.
- Does comparing numerals challenge them more than comparing number of objects?
- What strategies do they have to compare the two numerals?
- When given two sets, can they tell a story to compare the two sets, using appropriate comparative language and show clearly the difference between the two sets?

Extend:

Task A (Individual, Whole Group):

- Give the following directions:
  - If you have a brother, take a red cube.
  - If you do not have a brother, take a blue cube.
- Those with red cubes join their cubes to make a red tower; all with blue cubes make a blue tower. Display the two towers.
- Ask the following questions:
  - How many children have brothers? How do you know?
  - How many children do not have brothers? How do you know?
  - Are there more children without a brother than with a brother?
  - How many more? How many fewer? How do you know?
- Repeat this task for sisters.

Task B (Partners):

- Play **A Game of Capture.** This time the child with the largest number takes the number of counters that is the difference between the two numbers on the cards—for example, the first child turns over a 4, and the second child turns over a 7; then the second child takes 3 counters and lays in a pile. When all cards are turned over each child counts his or her counters and compares totals. One with the greater number of counters is the winner.

Task C (Whole Group):

- **Task** involves comparing more than two set of objects and uses the words *greatest* and *least number.* Take time to ensure children understand and can use these words.
- Ask the following:
  - Count how many pockets you have, and print that number on an index card.

- o The child with the greatest number of pockets stands in front of group.
- o The child with the least number of pockets stands in front of group.
- o Who has more? How many more?
- Share strategies used to find the difference—for example, do they use the counting up strategy? Do they count backwards? Do they use fingers? Do they know from memory?

Reflection and Discussion:

Children (Individual, Whole Group, Teacher-Posed Questions):

- Which activities did you like: The ones you had to find more than or fewer than? Why?
- In some games, there was a winner. Do you like playing these types of math games? Why? Why not?
- Do you think learning about more than and fewer than is useful in your life outside of school? Why?

Teacher(s) (If possible, discuss your reflections with colleagues.):

- Some children find the concept of "fewer than" more difficult than "more than." Have you found this to be so during this **Investigation**? If so, why do you think so? What could you do to help children learn the "fewer than" concept?
- Several of the tasks had games where there were winners. What do you think about that? Is it a level of competitiveness that lends to a positive learning experience for young children?
- There is an emphasis on using the mathematical comparative language. Were your children comfortable in using this language to compare quantities and numbers?

Note: How Many Snails? A Counting Book **Investigation B** focuses on comparing numbers but also includes the comparison symbolism of <, >, =, and writing inequalities.

COMPARING NUMBERS

How Many Snails? A Counting Book

Paul Giganti Jr.

Illustrated by Donald Crews

Summary: An intriguing book to ponder and deliberate deeply and tax one's visual discrimination skills in order to determine "how many in a set and part of a set." Throughout *How Many Snails? A Counting Book,* Giganti asks increasingly more challenging "How many . . ." questions about common things in nature—for example, clouds, flowers, snails; the numbers of books in a library; cupcakes in a bakery; and dogs in the park. Written in a repetitive questioning format, Giganti poses three "how many" questions for each familiar object, requiring one to compare objects in order to answer the questions. Such questions compel one to look carefully at each of Donald Crews's bold, bright gouache double-page spreads to find the answers.

Note: How Many Snails? A Counting Book *was introduced to children in the* How Many Snails? A Counting Book ***Investigation A*** (see Unit I). *Now it is being used to develop other **Learning Expectations** related to comparison of numbers.*

INVESTIGATION B—I WONDER HOW MANY MORE?

Mathematics and Literature Experiences

Learning Expectations:

- To compare sets of objects for more than, fewer than, and equal to the number of objects in another group
- To use appropriate language and symbolism to compare quantities and numbers less than 20
- To connect different representations of mathematical ideas
- To use spoken and written language to communicate coherently and effectively mathematical reasoning to various audiences

Learning Resources: Multiple copies of *How Many Snails? A Counting Book;* counters; chart paper, whiteboard, or overhead

Read Aloud (Whole Group, Teacher):

- Reread together *How Many Snails? A Counting Book.*

Note: *Each time a book is reread, new understandings are gained.*

Engage:

Task A (Small and Whole Groups):

- Give each small group a copy of *How Many Snails? A Counting Book.* Revisit the double-page spread depicting fish.
- Ask the following questions:
  - Are there more red fish with their mouths closed than with their mouths open?
    - Allow time for children to sort and count.
    - Expect children to tell there are more and how many more.
    - Encourage use of complete sentences when explaining their reasoning. Model verbally and in writing this language at first.

Here are some samples:

- There are more fish with their mouths open than with their mouths closed.
- There are 4 fish with their mouths open and 3 with their mouths closed. The number 4 is greater than 3, or 4 is 1 more than 3.
- Record symbolically, for example, $4 > 3$ and $4 = 3 + 1$. Relate symbolism to the illustrations and language. Allow time for children to question and discuss.

Task B (Whole Group):

- Refer to **Task A,** choose a child, and say, "[Child's name] said that there are fewer fish with their mouths closed than with their mouths open." Do you think he or she is right? Why?
- This should lead to a discussion of the comparative language and symbolism.
- Record symbolically 3 < 4 or 3 = 4 − 1. Allow time to discuss the symbolic representations and connect to the illustrations and language of comparison.

Task C (Whole Group):

- Repeat **Task B** for other fish or other objects depicted in the book—for example:
  o Are there more orange fish than yellow fish? How do you know? Share and record, as suggested previously. Share solutions.
  o Are there fewer tiny books than big books?

Engage Observations:

- How do they compare the two sets?
- How do they figure out how many more? What strategies do they use?
- Are they able to explain in sentences how they knew which set has more?
- Are the children able to record symbolically their solutions?
- Do they use comparative language appropriately?
- Can they see the relationship between more than and less than when written symbolically?

Explore:

Task A (Small Groups):

- Each group with a copy of *How Many Snails? A Counting Book* opens to the double-page spread with starfish.
- Ask the following questions:
  o Are there more starfish with five arms on the rocks or more starfish in the water?
  o How do you know?
- Children represent on paper how they know. Encourage writing of numerals to show how many of each starfish and how many more starfish are in the water. Encourage the children to write symbolic inequalities to show their solutions.
- Repeat **Task** with other illustrations—for example, cupcakes, comparing those with white icing and those with chocolate icing. Include questions such as Are there fewer cupcakes with brown icing than white icing (no sprinkles)?

Task B (Partners, Whole Group):

Center Activity

- Model this **Task** with the whole group before children go to the math center.
- Partners share a deck of number cards (1–9). Each has a recording sheet.
- Each child draws a card from the deck and compares the numbers—for example, one child says, "Mine is more than yours because 5 is more than 3." The other child may say, "Mine is less than yours because 3 is less than 5."
- Each child records the comparison symbolically on paper. They compare recordings.
- One child: 5 > 3   Partner: 3 < 5
- Repeat at least six times, using other cards.

Variation:

- Use two decks of number cards 0 to 9. (There is the possibility that numbers drawn are equal.)
- Use number cards 10 to 19 to compare larger numbers.

Explore Observations:

- How do the children keep track when comparing sets? Do they use numbers?
- Are they able to write > and < to show the relationships?
- When counting larger sets of objects (cupcakes), do they count by ones or skip count?
- Are they able to explain how they counted the objects? Do they accept that it can be done in different ways?
- Do they use appropriately comparative language?
- When comparing two numbers are they able to state the comparison using appropriate language and record the comparison using either < or >?

Consolidate:

Task A (Individual, Whole Group):

- Each child illustrates more snails without stripes than those with stripes. Encourage writing numerals and symbols to show the comparison. Share the illustration, using comparative language to describe the relationship.
- Repeat for other objects and using fewer instead of more.

Task B (Individual, Whole Group):

- Pose the following problems to the children:

(Refer to the illustration of snails.)

A. Tomi puts the striped snails into a fish bowl.

Jamie puts the snails that do not have stripes in another bowl.

Which bowl has more snails? How do you know?

- Show how solutions are found. Encourage drawings, words, and use of symbols.
- Share strategies used to find solutions.

B. (Refer to the illustration of dogs.)

Jane feeds all the dogs with their tongues out.

Jason feeds all the dogs that are brown.

Who has to feed fewer dogs? How do you know?

- Show how solutions are found. Encourage drawings, words, and use of symbols.
- Share strategies used to find solutions.

Task C (Partners, Whole Group):

What's My Number?

- Model the **Task** with the whole group (two children who know the game could model).
- Partners share a deck of number cards (0–9).
- One child draws a card and does not let the partner see it.
- Child gives clues using comparative language to help the partner guess the hidden number—for example, the child draws a 6 and may say, "My number is less than 8 but greater than 3." The partner writes down possible numbers, says, "It could be 4, 5, 6, or 7. Give me another clue." The child says, "It is less than 7 but greater than 5." The partner looks at the possible answers written down and says, "It must be 6."
- Partners switch roles.

Variation:

- Repeat the previous **Task** but use number cards 10 to 19.

Consolidate Observations:

- What strategies do the children use to illustrate pages? How do they keep track?
- Do they use numerals and comparison symbols to correspond to their illustrations? Are they accurate?
- How do they talk about sets that have the same number of objects? When asked how many more, are they able to say zero?
- What strategies are used to find a solution to the problem? Do they count the objects illustrated? Use counters? Do they write numerals and symbols to show relationship?
- Can they explain the strategies used to find a solution? Do they listen as other children explain their solutions and strategies?
- Are they giving clues appropriate for the number chosen? Are they using correct comparison language?

Extend:

Task A (Partners):

- Children choose something of interest from nature, home, bakery, or toy store as illustrated in *How Many Snails? A Counting Book*. Find books, websites, etc., about the object. Share factual information about "something of interest." Display the books, etc., and the information.

Task B (Individual, Whole Group):

- The dedication page states, "For all the people who count." What do you think the author means? Who might he be referring to?
- If you wrote this book, to whom would you dedicate it and why?

Task C (Partners):

- This task is for children who are ready to work with two digit numbers greater than 20.
- Model:
  - Roll two number cubes, numbered 1 to 6, and use the numbers rolled to form two 2-digit numbers. For example, if the numbers rolled are 3 and 5, record 35 and 53.
  - Record in symbolic form the relationship between the two numbers—for example, 35 < 53 or 53 > 35.
- Partners repeat five times and record.

Note: *If the number on the faces is the same—for example, 4 and 4, then the child would record 44 = 44.*

Reflection and Discussion:

Children (Individual, Whole Group, Teacher-Posed Questions):

- How did you keep track of the number of objects to draw so you have more in one set than the other? What strategies did you use?
- Did you find any of the **Tasks** challenging? Which one(s)? Why?
- What did you learn when you heard your classmates share how they found the solutions to the tasks?
- What did you like or not like about doing these tasks?

Teacher(s) (If possible, discuss responses with colleagues.):

- What particular problems did the **Investigation** pose for your children? Which parts were easiest for them?
- If some children had difficulty with this **Investigation,** how might you change it so it would be more successful?
- What challenges were presented when children were asked to use the language and symbols of comparison?
- If necessary, how could you change your instructional strategies so more children would accept the challenges presented in the tasks?
- Were all the children engaged in the **Investigation?** If not, why do you think they were not? What would you change to get them more involved?

NUMBERS THAT MAKE 10

Ten Flashing Fireflies

Philemon Sturges

Illustrated by Anna Rotech

Summary: "What do you see in the summer night?" For a young sister and brother, they are intrigued with "Ten flashing fireflies burning bright!" So they begin to capture each firefly, one by one, and place it in a jar. As they do so, they count, "One flashing firefly in our jar . . . Two flashing fireflies . . ." until they imprison all ten fireflies. At bedtime, they place the jar in their bedroom and observe the fireflies. As the fireflies' light flickers and fades, they decide to open the jar and release them. As they fly away, the children count down, 10 to 1. Throughout the text, one is challenged constantly to find the number that when added to a given number makes 10. Written in lyrical rhyming text, *Ten Flashing Fireflies* invites children to read along as the counting book unfolds. The dusty chalk double-page spreads depict well the nighttime colors and atmosphere, and embed creatively a number of nocturnal animals.

INVESTIGATION: WHAT DO WE SEE IN THE SUMMER NIGHT?

Mathematics and Literature Experiences

Learning Expectations:

- To find the number that makes 10, for any number from 1 to 9, when added to the given number, by using objects or drawings, and record the answer with a drawing or equation
- To see the relationship between missing addends and subtraction
- To model with mathematics and look for patterns to solve problems
- To recognize common types of texts—for example, poems
- To use illustrations to describe the setting
- To read poetry of appropriate complexity with prompting and support for grade level
- To become familiar with poetic language and structure

Learning Resources: Multiple copies of *Ten Flashing Fireflies*, **10-Frames**, counters, and multilink cubes

Read Aloud (Whole Group, Teacher as Reader):

- Explore and discuss the book jacket—title, author, illustrator, and illustration.
- After each double-page spread is read, allow time for the children to predict the next number.
- As the children become familiar with the poetic language and structure, invite them to **Read Aloud.**

- Reread *Ten Flashing Flies* and dramatize.
- Place copies of *Ten Flashing Flies* at the math center for independent, peer, and home reading.

Engage:

Task A (Whole Group):

- Revisit the first double-page spread of the ten fireflies.
- Ask the following questions:
  - How many fireflies do you see on the page?
  - If you did not know how many fireflies, what could you do to find out?
- Share solutions and how they know.

  Here are some samples:

  - "I counted them." Ask, How did you count?
  - Did anyone do it another way?
    - "I saw 4 and 3 and 3." "I saw 7 and 3." "I saw 5 and 5."

Task B (Whole Group):

Resource: Bright colored multilink cubes

- Dramatize the story by having 10 children (fireflies) hold a yellow, orange, or red linking cube. Another child (jar keeper) stands by with an open transparent jar.
- Other children (the audience) watch the actions of the 10 children and the jar as the story is dramatized but participate in finding and checking answers.
- Read the first page: "What do we see . . . ten flashing fireflies, burning bright!" Audience counts the number of firefly actors, double-checking there are 10, who "flash" around showing their colored multilink cube.
- Read, "Catch the one twinkling there...." The jar keeper captures one multilink cube, drops it in the jar, and joins the audience.
- Read, "One flashing firefly in our jar."
- Ask the following questions:
  - How many flashing fireflies in *our* jar? In the sky? Audience tells how many and how they know.
- Say together, "One in the jar and 9 in the sky" or "9 in the sky and 1 in the jar. Altogether there are 10 fireflies."
- Repeat for remaining pages until 10 fireflies are in the jar and none in the sky.
- Say, "There are zero fireflies in the sky."
- Repeat with another 11 actors/actresses.
- Ask the following questions:
  - What do you notice about the number of fireflies in the jar?
  - What do you notice about the number of fireflies in the sky?

Engage Observations:

- What strategies do children use to determine the number of fireflies? Do they do the following?
    - Count by ones by touching each firefly?
    - Subitize and add small groups together?
    - Place counters on the flies to count?
    - Double-check their counting?
- Are children accurate in their counting?
- Do they see the relationship between the number of fireflies in the jar and the number in the sky (sum to 10) and use it as a strategy for finding the number of each?

Explore:

Task A (Partners, Whole Group):

Resources: Copies of *Ten Flashing Fireflies* and large recording sheet: **Fireflies** (Appendix B [1])

- Read together each double-page spread, and together determine how many fireflies are in the jar and how many are in the sky and why.
- Take turns recording in the first two columns.

Fireflies

In the Summer Night	In the Jar	Equation
10	0	
9	1	
. .		
0		

- When completed, partners discuss what they notice about the recorded numbers.
- Ask the following question:
    - What patterns do you see?
- Share and record responses with whole group.

Here are some samples:

- In the "in the summer night" column, numbers go down from 10 to 0, and "in the jar" column numbers go up from 0 to 10.
- The numbers across the line add to 10.
- If you know the number in the sky, you can tell how many are in the jar.

- After each observation, ask the following question:
  - How do you know, or why do you think that is so?
- Together write equations for each row of the recording sheet and record in the third column.

Example: $10 + 0 = 10 \ldots \quad 0 + 10 = 10$

Task B (Partners, Whole Group):

Resources: Recording sheet: **Fireflies** (Appendix B [1])

- Present the recording sheet: **Fireflies.** Post a large recording sheet: **Fireflies** for group sharing of answers.

Fireflies

In the Summer Night	In the Jar	Equations
10		
	1	
	2	
7		
	5	
4		
3		
	8	
1		
0		

- Together complete a row—for example, point to the row with 7 in left-hand column.
- Ask the following question:
  - How could we find the missing number in this row (in the jar)?

Note: *Counting down the columns and following the pattern are legitimate ways of finding the missing number. However, there are other ways to find the missing number.*

  - Are there other ways to find the missing number?
- Record solutions.

Here is a sample:

  - Since the total number of fireflies is 10 then we need to find how many to add to 7 to get 10.
- Ask the following questions:
  - How could you find that number?

Here are some sample answers:

□ You can count on: 7. . . , 8, 9, 10. You add 3.
□ You subtract 7 from 10; that is 3.

- Together record the equation for each strategy: $7 + \square = 10$; $10 - 7 = \square$.
- Compare and discuss the two equations; how $10 - 7 = \square$ can be used to find the unknown $\square$ in the equation $7 + \square = 10$.
- Partners find all unknown numbers and equations.
- Share, record, and discuss all strategies used.

Task C (Partners):

Resources: 10-Frame (Appendix E [1]) and counters

- State, "There are 7 fireflies. Show on your frame." Use counters to represent the fireflies on the **10-Frame.** Partner checks.

- Ask the following questions:
  o How many fireflies do we need to fill the frame? To make 10?

- After suggestions and agreement that it is 3, children add the counters.
- Write an equation to show how many you need to add to 7 to get 10.
- Together, write the equation: $7 + \square = 10$, relating to the **10-Frame.**
- Ask the following questions:
  o What number do we write in the $\square$?
  o How could you find it if you did not have the **10-Frame**? Discuss as before the counting on and subtraction strategies.
- Repeat for different start numbers between 1 and 9.

Note: *If children are comfortable with 0, you can use numbers between 0 and 10.*

Explore Observations:

- Are the children able to record numbers in the appropriate place on the chart?
- Are they able to relate recordings in the chart to the story and use the recordings to answer the questions posed?
- Are they able to see the relationship between the missing addend equation and corresponding subtraction equation?
- What strategies do they use to solve missing addend equations?
- Do they associate the missing addend equation with actions on the **10-Frame?**
- How do they use the **10-Frame** to find the unknown in a missing addend equation?

Consolidate:

Task A (Individual, Partners, Whole Group):

Resource: Recording sheet: **Make 10** (Appendix B [2])

- Provide each child with **Make 10** to complete.
- When completed share answers and strategies used to find the answers with the whole group.
- For those who say, "I just know," ask them to explain to someone who does not know how to find the answer.

Task B (Individual, Whole Group):

Resource: Recording sheet: **Matching** (Appendix B [3])

- When **Matching** is completed, share the strategies used to find the answers.

Task C (Individual, Whole Group):

Word Problems

Resources: Counters and **10-Frame** (Appendix E [1])

- Write word problems on index cards.
  - A. There are 10 fireflies in the evening sky. Minnie captures 3 and puts them in the jar. How many are still in the sky?

  - B. There are 10 fireflies in the sky. Some of them are captured and put in the jar. Now there are 5 fireflies in the sky. How many are captured?

  - C. There are 10 fireflies in the sky. Now I see 2 fireflies inside the jar. How many are captured?

- Record solutions using drawings, words, and equations. Share solutions, using the following questions to promote discussion:
  - What is the solution? How did you find this?
  - Do you agree with what she said?
  - Did anyone do it differently? Tell us how.
  - Do you agree with what she said? Why?
  - Can you show us with the counters?
  - Does it make sense to you now?

Consolidate Observations:

- What strategies do they use to find the unknown in the equations?
- Are they able to explain to others the strategies they used?

(Continued)

(Continued)

- Can they learn from the explanations of others?
- Are they fluent in writing subtraction equations for the missing addend equations?
- Are they able to explain to others the solution strategies they used to solve the word problems?
- Are they able to write an equation to show how they solved the problem?

Extend:

Task A:

- Ask the following questions:
  o Have you ever seen a firefly?
  o Did you wonder how they light up?
- Research how fireflies light up.
- Share and discuss findings.

Reflection and Discussion:

Children (Individual, Whole Group, Teacher-Posed Questions):

- Your cousin asks you if you liked the book and why. What would you tell her?
- What parts of this **Investigation** did you like? Why?
- What strategies do you use to find the missing number in a missing addend equation?

Teacher(s) (If possible, share and discuss responses with colleagues.):

- How successful was the lesson? Did the children learn what you intended them to learn? How do you know?
- Was the book *Ten Flashing Fireflies* helpful in allowing the children to find numbers that make 10? In what way?
- Do you have other instructional strategies to help children understand that, for example, $10 - 7 = \Box$ and $7 + \Box = 10$ are equivalent equations?

ODD AND EVEN NUMBERS

365 Penguins

Jean-Luc Fromental

Illustrated by Joelle Jolivet

Summary: Imagine living with 365 penguins! How would you feed all of them, where would they all sleep, how would you look after them, how would you organize them . . . ? Well, such becomes the reality for one family—Mom, Dad, Amy, and her young brother (narrator). It all begins at nine o'clock on New Year's Day when the deliveryman brings a box which contains a penguin. Who sent it? Who attached the note, "I'm number 1. Feed me when I'm hungry."

However, the delivery does not stop there. The next day another penguin is delivered with an attached note. At first, the family sees the penguins as cute and gives each a name. BUT, the penguins continue to be delivered for a whole year! As they mount up, the family is faced with the monumental task of cleaning, feeding, naming, and housing them. To the rescue is Uncle Victor, an ecologist, who arrives on the scene the following New Year's Eve and solves the mystery. While this humorous, engaging oversize picture book focuses on the concept of global warming, as well, it integrates meaningfully the mathematical concepts of odd and even numbers. Jolivet's entertaining illustrations of orange, blue, gray, black, and white vibrant hues on a white background complements fittingly the storyline.

INVESTIGATION: DO I HAVE A PARTNER?

Mathematics and Literature Experiences

Learning Expectations:

- To determine whether a group of objects has an odd or even number of members
- To determine whether the sum of two even numbers, sum of two odd numbers, and sum of an even and an odd number is even or odd and to explain why
- To make a generalization
- To identify who is telling/narrating the story
- To listen to stories to instill a sense of story
- To increase cognitive skills, including the ability to think critically

Learning Resource: Multiple copies of *365 Penguins*

Read Aloud (Whole Group, Teacher as Reader):

- Discuss the book jacket—its title, author, illustrator, and illustrations.
- Share the overview of the story cited on the back of the book jacket and why such is written.
- **Read Aloud** the story, allowing time for the children to view the illustrations, noting the writing style, and comprehending the unfolding saga.
- At the completion of the story, share thoughts on what might happen next.
- Place copies of *365 Penguins* in the math center.

Note: *You may need to reread* 365 Penguins *before engaging in the* **Investigation**.

Engage:

Task A (Partners, Whole Group):

- Read together the fifth double-page spread, "What should we do with all the penguins?"
- Ask for suggestions. If you get no responses, then suggest that one member of the family wants to line the penguins up in 2s and have them march in a parade. Everyone would have a partner.

- Ask the following question:
  - Can that happen if we have (state number of children in group) penguins? I wonder!
- Model what it means to have a partner and what it means to have one left over.
- Invite six children to line up in 2s.
- Ask the following question:
  - Does everyone have a partner? Discuss.
- Invite five children to line up in 2s.
- Ask the following question:
  - Does everyone have a partner? Discuss, noting that everyone has a partner but one. Introduce language of *one left over*.
- Solve together:
  - If the family wants the penguins to have a partner to march in the parade, on which days would the penguins be lined up with a partner? Start with Day 1.
- Ask children to pretend they are penguins to find the solution.
- As children line up record findings for each day in the following chart.

Here are some examples:

- Day 1: 1 child. Do you have a partner? Record.
- Day 2: How many penguins? How do we know? (Relate to the story that one new penguin arrives each day.) One child joins the one already standing. Do the penguins have a partner? Children arrange themselves. Are there any left over? Record.
- Day 3: How many penguins? Again ask why relating to story. They agree there are 3 children since 1 more joins the 2 that are there. Can we line up in 2s? Children arrange themselves. Are there any left over? Continue until all children have a partner, determining if any left over or not.

Day	Number of Penguins	Penguin Has a Partner	One Left Over
1	1	no	yes
2	2	yes	no
	3	no	yes
Note: *Continue to Day 20 or number of people in the group.*			
20 (or number of people in group)	20	yes	no

- Partners share what they notice about the numbers.
- Share with the whole group.

Here are some sample responses:

- o The number of days and number of penguins are the same. Allow time to explain why this is so (refer back to the story).
- o The numbers 2, 4, 6, 8 . . . all have partners.
- o The numbers 2, 4, 6, 8 . . . all have friends.
- o The numbers 2, 4, 6, 8 . . . can be lined up in 2s.
- o The numbers 1, 3, 5 . . . have one left over when they line up in 2s.
- o The numbers 2, 4, 6 . . . do not have any left over; they can form groups of two with no penguins walking by themselves.
- o When a number does not have a partner, it has one left over.

Task B (Individual, Partners):

Resources: 100s Chart (Appendix E [2]), colored pencils, and counters

Note: *This **Task** is done after **Task A** is completed.*

- • Provide each child with a **100s Chart**. Color yellow the numbers with partners (2, 4, 6, 8 . . .); color green the numbers with one left over (1, 3, 5, 7 . . .) up to the number of penguins recorded in the table in **Task A.**
  - o As you read together the numbers shaded yellow, what do you notice? Does anyone notice anything different?
- • Repeat for numbers shaded green.
- • Ask the following questions:
  - o Does anyone know the names we give to these two sets of numbers?
  - o Write the words *even* and *odd*.
  - o Why do you think this set (pointing to and saying together the even numbers on the table) is called even? Why is this set (pointing to and saying together the odd ones) called odd?
  - o Relate even numbers to numbers with partners and odd numbers to those who have one left over when grouped in 2s.
- • Ask the following questions:
  - o Look at your **100s Chart.** Find the number 33. Circle it. Would you color it yellow or green? Why? Why not?
  - o Is 33 even or odd? How do you know?
  - o Continue shading even and odd numbers to 50 (yellow or green).
  - o How did you know which numbers to color yellow? Color green?

Task C [Individual, Whole Group]:

- • Relate odd and even numbers to children's lived world—for example, house numbers: odds on one side of street and evens on the other. Children share their own house numbers. Record in a table.
- • At what other events in your life do you use even and odd numbers?

Engage Observations:

- Do children recognize the difference between numbers (represented by children and shading on a **100s Chart**) that can be grouped in 2s with no leftovers and those when grouped by 2s that have one left over?
- What patterns do children recognize for even numbers on **100s Chart**? For odd numbers?
- Can children describe even numbers? Odd numbers?
- How do they determine if numbers higher than the ones shaded on the table are even or odd? Do they use a rule? Do they have to use the **100s Chart**?

Explore:

Task A (Partners):

Resources: Square tiles, **100s Chart** (Appendix E [2]), and recording sheet: **Lining Up Tiles** (Appendix B [4])

- Ask:
  - o Line up the tiles in 2s, starting at Day 1 and finishing on Day 20.
  - o Record the days when the tiles can be lined up in 2s with none left over and the days when there will be one left over.

Lining Up Tiles

Day	Number of tiles	Every tile can be lined up in 2s with none left over.	One left over
1	1		
2	2		
3	3		
‘ ‘ ‘			
20			

- Ask the children to do the following and ask the following questions:
  - o Write the numbers that do not have any left over when arranged in 2s.
  - o Write the numbers that have one left over when arranged in 2s.

o If someone asked you what an even number is, what would you say?

o If someone asked you what an odd number is, what would you say?

o Could you tell them how you know if a number is even or odd without arranging them in groups of 2s? Discuss.

o Is 69 even or odd? How do you know?

o Is 98 even or odd? How do you know?

Task B (Individual, Partners):

Resource: Recording sheet: **Adding Even Numbers** (Appendix B [5])

- Ask the following question:

  o What do you predict? If you add two even numbers will the answer be even or odd?

- Allow time to share predictions and why.

- Provide partners with a recording sheet: **Adding Even Numbers**. Ask the following questions:

  o What do you notice about the numbers on the top row?

  o What do you notice about the numbers in the first column?

  o What are you asked to do with the numbers?

- Partners help each other and check each other's sums.

- Ask and discuss the following questions:

  o What was the same about the numbers we added?

  o What do we notice about the sums? How did you know?

  o Was your prediction correct?

  o Have you changed your thinking?

  o We notice that when we added two even numbers the sum is even. Can you explain why? Can you show why, using the tiles?

  o Will it always work? How do you know?

- Partners, using **100s Chart,** choose any two even numbers less than 50. Add them. Is the sum even? Each partner takes three more turns.

- Share findings; write the rule for adding two even numbers and share with class.

Task C (Individual, Whole Group):

- What do you predict if you add two odd numbers? Will the sum be even or odd?

- Make and justify predictions.

- Provide partners with a recording sheet: **Adding Odd Numbers** (Appendix B [6]) to complete.

- Before beginning to complete, ask questions as in **Task B.**

- Share when the sheet is completed:

  o What is the same about the numbers we added?

  o What do we notice about the sums? How do you know that is true?

  o Is your prediction correct?

  o Have you changed your thinking?

  o When you add two odd numbers is the sum even? Show using the tiles.

  o Does this rule always work? How do you know?

- Partners choose any two odd numbers less than 50 and find the sum. Circle the sum on the **100s Chart.** Is it even or odd?
- Take three turns each.
- Share findings. Write and share the rule.

Explore Observations:

- Are the children able to arrange the tiles in groups of two and record results?
- Are they able to read the table?
- Can they distinguish between even and odd numbers?
- Can they describe in words an odd number? An even number?
- Can they explain in words the results of adding two even numbers? Two odd numbers?
- Can they justify this same result using the tiles?
- Can they apply the rule to numbers not included in the table? Can they do it without adding the numbers?

Consolidate:

Task A (Individual, Whole Group):

- What do you predict if you add an even and odd number? Will the sum be even or odd?
- Share and justify predictions.
- Prove to a partner that your prediction is correct.
- Present answers and explain reasoning.
- Share the general rule for adding an even and odd number and record:

"The sum of an even and odd number is odd."

- Ask the following question:
  o Does it make a difference if you add an odd number to an even number? Allow time to justify their reasoning.
- Ask the following question:
  o If you add 26 plus 33, is the answer even or odd? If you add 37 plus 22? How do you know?
  o Repeat for other examples.

Task B (Whole Group):

- Determine if the answer is even or odd. Share with the whole class why you know.

Note: *Encourage children to apply the rules for adding even and odd numbers, rather than actually adding the numbers and determining if the sum is even or odd.*

A. 19 + 33 _____

B. 22 + 45 _____

C. 46 + 12 _____

D. 13 + 52 _____

Consolidate Observations:

- How do children organize their work to determine if adding an even and odd number is odd?
- How do they rationalize that the result is the same when you add an even and odd number or an odd or even number?
- What strategies do they use to add even and odd numbers when written symbolically?
- Can they determine whether the sum of two numbers is odd or even without actually finding the sum?

Extend:

Task A (Individual, Whole Group):

- Read together, "364 . . . 365 . . . You're all here, my dears. Even you, my little Chilly, with your blue feet."
- Ask the following questions:
  - What do you think? Is there an even or odd number of penguins?
  - How do you know?
- Share reasons.
- Read together, "Then Uncle Victor explained to us . . . Your old Uncle Victor is not so crazy."
- Ask the following question:
  - How do you think this tells us that 365 is an odd number?

Task B (Individual, Whole Group):

- Twenty penguins are marching.
- Ask the following question:
  - How many different ways can all 20 penguins line up so that there is no penguin marching alone?
- Use counters to help find your solution.
- Show your solution using words, diagrams, and numbers.

Task C (Individual, Partners):

- Choose a page from *365 Penguins;* write a word problem related to the words and illustrations on the page.
- Partners share problems and solve.

Task D (Individual):

- Check if children can tell if the sum of two numbers is even or odd when the sum is not obvious to them (e.g., add 2598 + 4673).

Reflection and Discussion:

Children (Individual, Whole Group, Teacher-Posed Questions):

- Did you find this **Investigation** interesting?
- What did you like best about the book?
- Why did the author add the penguin with the blue feet?
- If you were writing to your cousin what would you tell her was the most interesting part of the book?

Teacher(s) (If possible, share and discuss responses with colleagues.):

- Did this lesson help children understand the difference between odd and even numbers?
- Can you share another lesson that would help develop the concept of odd and even numbers?
- Was the **Investigation** effective in developing the rules for determining the sum when adding odd and even numbers?
- Was there sufficient time allotted in the **Investigation** for children to communicate with each other as partners or in whole group? What changes might you make if you were to use it again?
- Were there sufficient suggestions given to have children use different forms of communication, such as, writing, listening, speaking? What would you add?
- What instructional strategies do you have to motivate children to share their reasoning?
- Were the children willing to take risks when making predictions?

SKIP COUNTING BY 2s, 5s, AND 10s

Two Ways to Count to Ten: A Liberian Folktale

Retold by Ruby Dee

Illustrated by Susan Meddaugh

Summary: This is a retelling of the Liberian folktale about the powerful, wise King Leopard, who is dying and needs to find a worthy successor. His successor must be the cleverest of beasts, wise to rule and also be a prince for his daughter. In time, he and the king's daughter will become king and queen. But, how will the king choose his successor? Once his decision is made, he calls all the animals together and shares his plan. With the king's spear, each animal is to throw it into the air. "He must throw it so high that he can count to ten before it comes down again." However, King Leopard does not share ways as to how the count is to be done. The contest begins. Who will win?

What are the different ways to count to 10? What is the quickest way to count to 10? The color-pencil and watercolor double-page illustrations depict well this simple, direct plot and create a personality for each animal.

INVESTIGATION: THE ANTELOPE WON!

Mathematics and Literature Experiences

Learning Expectations:

- To skip count orally by 2s, 5s, and 10s to 100
- To use skip counting to count a number of objects
- To communicate reasoning to others
- To determine the central message, lesson, or moral of a folktale
- To read literary texts in a variety of genres

Learning Resources: Multiple copies of *Two Ways to Count to Ten: A Liberian Folktale*; **100s Chart**; floor model number lines divided by 2s, 5s, and 10s; counters

Read Aloud (Whole Group, Teacher as Reader):

- Explore and discuss the book jacket—its title, author, illustrator, and illustration.
- In your conversation about the author, discuss "retold by" Ruby Dee.
- Define and discuss what a folktale is.
- Share titles of other folktales, and have samples available.
- Using a map, globe, etc., to locate Liberia—setting for *Two Ways to Count to Ten*.
- Read the entire folktale, providing time for the children to view the illustrations and to predict what animal may follow the preceding animal—and why.
- Place multiple copies of *Two Ways to Count to Ten* in the math center and, if available, other folktales to spark children's interest in this literary genre.

Engage:

Task A (Partners, Whole Group):

- Read (fourth double-page spread), "He flung the spear far up into the air and caught it . . . . He must send it so high that he can count to ten before it comes down again."
- Read (thirteenth and fourteenth double-page spread), "With a toss of his head, he flung the spear far up into the air . . . he called out five words. "Two! Four! Six! Eight! Ten! he cried."
- The children will discuss with a partner the following:
  o How did the antelope count to ten?
  o Do you think what the antelope did was fair?
  o Why was the antelope chosen to be the prince?
- Share answers and reasoning with the whole group.

Task B (Partners, Whole Group):

- Ask the following question:
  - o Are there other ways the antelope could have counted to 10?
- Partners share possible ways.
- Share suggestions with the whole group. As they share, children recite the count suggested—for example:
  - o Count by 1s: 1, 2, 3 . . . 8, 9, 10
  - o Count by 5s: 5, 10
- Record the possible ways and the counts.
- Ask the following questions:
  - o Do you think the antelope should have chosen one of these ways to count?
  - o Why do you think he didn't?
- Discuss the title *Two Ways to Count to Ten.*
- Ask the following questions:
  - o Why do you think the folktale is titled *Two Ways to Count to Ten?*
  - o Is it an appropriate title for the tale? Why or why not?
  - o Can you count to 10 by 3s? Why or why not?
- Share and discuss reasons.

Engage Observations:

- Can the children relate the skip counting by 2s to what the antelope did in the story?
- Do children recognize that counting by 1s, counting by 2s, and counting by 5s are ways to count to 10?
- How do children figure out that you cannot skip count by 3s to reach 10? Can they explain their reasoning?

Explore:

Task A (Partners):

Resource: Counters

- Suppose the king had decided that in order to be prince you had to count to 20.
- Ask the following question:
  - o How might the antelope have done that?

Note: *Twenty counters should be available if children need them to skip count to 20.*

- Share answers and how they were found.
- Record all the ways suggested—for example:
  - o 1s: 1, 2, 3, 4 . . . 18, 19, 20
  - o 2s: 2, 4, 6 . . . 16, 18, 20
  - o 4s : 4, 8, 12, 16, 20
  - o 5s : 5, 10, 15, 20
  - o 10s: 10, 20

- Ask the following question:
  - ○ Which would be the best way for the antelope to count to 20? Justify the choice.
- Ask the following question:
  - ○ Can you skip count to 20 using 3s? Explain why or why not.

Task B (Whole Group):

- Ask the following question:
  - ○ When is skip counting important, and why?
- Share responses.
- Ask the following questions:
  - ○ What objects in the classroom could we count using skip counting? Record.
  - ○ How many eyes do you think there are in our whole group?
- Children stand in a line; one child points as all chant in unison:
  - ○ 2, 4, 6, 8, 10, 12, 14, 16, 18, 20, 22 . . . until all eyes are counted.
- Ask the following question:
  - ○ If we count all the eyes by ones, how many would there be?
- Share answers and why.

Note: *Do any of the children need to recount by ones to ensure the exact number of eyes? Recognize that counting by 2s gives the same count as counting by 1s is a difficult concept for some children. They need many experiences counting both ways to allow for development of a deep understanding of this important concept.*

- Repeat the previous **Task** by doing the following:
  - ○ Counting fingers by 5s
  - ○ Fingers on both hands by 10s
- Ask the following question:
  - ○ What other equal groups can be counted by skip counting by 5s and 10s?

Task C (Individual, Partners, Whole Group):

Resources: Large **100s Chart** (Appendix E [2]), sheet with **Four 100s Chart** (Appendix B [7]), and crayons or colored pencils

- On a large **100s Chart,** together skip count by 5s—for example, mark 5, then count 5 more, land on 10; count 5 more, land on 15, etc., highlighting the numbers skipped over and the numbers landed on. Continue to 50.
- Ask the following questions:
  - ○ How many numbers do you count when we move from 5 to 10? 10 to 15? 15 to 20, etc.?
- Repeat, and have children clap each time a multiple of 5 is said.
- Provide each child with a copy of the **Four 100s Chart.**

  Sheet 1: Starting at 2, skip count to 30. Color the squares red.

  Sheet 2: Starting at 5, skip count to 30. Color blue.

Sheet 3: Starting at 10, skip count to 30. Color yellow.

Sheet 4: Child's choice

- When the charts are completed, ask the following question:
  - What patterns do you notice on each sheet? Share with your partner.
- Share and compare patterns with whole group.
- Ask the children to do the following:
  - Use the patterns found to complete each chart to 100. Partners check each other's work.

Task D (Whole Group):

- Floor number lines labeled and fastened to floor:

Number Line A. 0, 2, 4, 6 . . . 20

Number Line B. 0, 5, 10, 15 . . . 20

Number Line C. 0, 10, 20, 30, 40, 50, 60, 70, 80, 90, 100

- One child stands at 0 and then hops on the numbers; others chant the numbers.
- Repeat throughout the year using different number lines.

Explore Observations:

- Can children find all the ways to skip count to 20? Or do they give up after finding one or two?
- Do they listen to the ideas of others?
- Do they make use of the counters to help with the skip counting?
- Can they justify why skip counting by certain numbers is better than others?
- Can children use skip counting to count a number of objects?
- Do the children realize that counting a number of objects by skip counting gives the same total count as if you counted by 1s?
- Can children use the patterns formed on the **100s Chart** when skip counting to 50 to continue the counting to 100?
- When sharing patterns on **100s Chart** do they describe them geometrically or numerically, or both?
- Are children able to say the numbers as they hop on the number line?

Consolidate:

Task A (Partners):

Center Task

Resources: Labeled containers with objects (between 20 and 100) and **How Many?** (Appendix B [8])

- At a center, partners choose a container and complete a recording sheet: **How Many?**
- Demonstrate procedure for completing sheet with whole group.

- When partners have completed the sheet, share and discuss answers with whole group.

Task B (Individual, Whole Group):

- Ask the following questions:
  - o Can you count to 48 by 2s?
  - o Share solutions. Can you explain how the counting was done?
  - o Can you count to 60 by 5s? by 10s?
  - o Can you count to 48 by 3s? why or why not?

Task C: (Partners)

Resource: 100s Chart (Appendix E [2]), **Numbers in Common** (Appendix B [9])

- Assign partners the **Numbers in Common.** When completed, share and discuss answers with the whole group.

Consolidate Observations:

- Are children counting sets of objects accurately when using skip counting?
- Are children fluent in skip counting by 2s, 5s, and 10s to certain numbers and without the use of counters or **100s Chart**?
- Are the children able to list the numbers named when they count by 2s and by 5s and pick out the numbers that are named in both lists?
- Are the children able to write their own problem similar to the one in **Task C**?

Extend:

Task A (Individual):

Resource: 100s Chart (Appendix E [2])

- Ask the children to do the following:
  - o Using **100s Chart,** count by 10s starting at 5. Record numbers counted.
  - o What do you notice about the numbers?
- Repeat for counting by 2s, starting at 1.
- Repeat counting by 2s and 10s using different start numbers.

Task B:

Resource: 100s Chart (Appendix E [2])

- Ask the children to do the following:
  - o Using a **100s Chart,** find all the numbers that you can use to skip count to 100. Record the numbers and the numbers counted to reach 100 on the **100s Chart.**

Here is a sample:

  - o Counting by 4s: 4, 8, 12, 16, 20, 24, 28, 32, 36, 40, 44, 48, 52, 56, 60, 64, 68, 72, 76, 80, 84, 88, 92, 96, 100

Reflection and Discussion:

Children (Individual, Whole Group, Teacher-Posed Questions):

- Who was your favorite animal in the story? Why?
- The king called the antelope the cleverest of the animals. Why do you think he said that?
- Do you ever use skip counting at home? When?
- What parts of this **Investigation** were most challenging for you? Was your partner helpful to you? Did you learn from answers shared by other children?
- What did you think of the king's plan to choose a successor and husband for his daughter?
- What rules would you have for selecting a new king?

Teacher(s) (If possible, share and discuss responses with colleagues.):

- Did your children find this **Investigation** challenging? In what way(s)?
- Were there parts of this lesson you would have done differently? Why? What modifications or adjustments would you have made?
- Are your children able to explain the reasoning for their answers to others?
- Do they listen to the reasoning of others? Do they learn from it?

DOUBLING NUMBERS

Minnie's Diner: A Multiplying Menu

Dayle Ann Dodds

Illustrated by John Manders

Summary: A captivating, humorous story created around the mathematical concepts of doubling, patterning, and multiplication that entertains as well as educates! The McFay farming family includes Papa and his five sons. When farming, the sons are told constantly by Papa, "There'll be no eatin' till your work is through." However, the delicious aroma from Minnie's Diner drifts by, and it's too great for the sons to resist. They know there is no finer scrumptious food than from Minnie's kitchen. Without hesitation Will, the youngest and smallest, races to Minnie's and places his order, "1 soup, 1 salad, 1 sandwich some fries, and 1 of her special hot cherry pies." Before long, Bill, who is twice the size of Will, heads to the diner and says, "I'll have what Will has, but make it a double." The other brothers follow, placing the orders, twice the size of the previous brother's. Just as Dill, the oldest, receives his tray of 16 portions of each item, Papa McFay enters the diner to chastise his sons for not doing their chores. But the aroma is too great for him, so he orders double that of Dill's! Written in rhyming couplets with varied font sizes for emphasis and comical, cartoonlike gouache illustrations, this delightful story is pleasing and satisfying.

INVESTIGATION: WHAT HAPPENS WHEN YOU DOUBLE?

Mathematics and Mathematics Experiences

Learning Expectations:

- To relate doubling to addition and multiplication by 2
- To compare doubling to adding 2 to a number
- To use patterns to solve problems
- To communicate reasoning to others
- To develop a sense of story
- To identify characters, settings, and key events in a story
- To relate illustrations to the overall story in which they appear

Learning Resources: Multiple copies of *Minnie's Diner: A Multiplying Menu* and counters

Read Aloud (Whole Group, Teacher as Reader):

- Read the title, and view the book jacket's illustration. Have children predict what the story may be about from the book jacket and why.
- Discuss the meaning of "diner" and what other names are given to such a place. Share the names of diners they may know and why they are called diners. Record responses.
- Read the author's and illustrator's names; discuss their roles.
- Read and enjoy the story for its content, language, and power to ignite the children's imaginations.
- Place multiple copies of *Minnie's Diner: A Multiplying Menu* in the math center for independent, peer, and home reading.

Engage (Whole Group):

- Read together up to the following: "I'll have what Will has, but make it a double."
- Draw attention to Minnie and her tray of 2 specials.
- Ask the following questions:
  - Why does Minnie fill the tray with 2 specials?
  - Do you think Bill is served a double? How do you know?
- Ask the children to do the following:
  - Write an equation to show that the double Bill receives is the same as 2 specials.
  - Answer: $1 + 1 = 2$
- Discuss what double means and what it means to double a number.
- Continue to read together until "I'll have what Bill has, but make it a double."
- Ask the following questions:
  - How many specials of cherry pie will Phil get?
  - How do you know? Share and show solutions.

Note: *Children may remember the answer from the story. If so, ask them how they would know if it were not written or illustrated in the book.*

- Write an equation that would help Minnie find out how many cherry pies she has to serve Phil?   Answer: 2 + 2 = 4

Note: *Some children may suggest writing a multiplication equation for doubling:*

$$2 \times 2 = 4$$

*Record and recognize that it is another way, but symbolism of multiplication will not be formally dealt with in this **Investigation.***

- Continue the same questioning for Gill and Dill. Share and show solutions.

Engage Observations:

- Are children familiar with the idea of doubling? Can they relate it to their experiences?
- How do children show that doubling is the same as 2 specials? 4 specials? 8 specials? 16 specials? Do they use counters, make drawings, add, or find the answer in the book?
- Can they explain to the group how they found their solutions?
- Are they able to write equations to show how the numbers doubled? Can they relate the equation to the language and concept of doubling and the illustrations in the book?
- Are the children amazed at how large the numbers get when they are doubled?

Explore:

Task A (Individual, Partners, Whole Group):

- When Papa McFay gives his order, he wants double what Dill ordered. How many cherry pies did Minnie have to serve Papa? Allow children to first make predictions and then share how they were made.
- Check predictions using drawings and numbers. Those who wish to do so can use counters.
- Make a group chart, and record the number of cherry pies each character is served:

Will	Bill	Phil	Gill	Dill	Papa
1	2	4	8	16	32

- Refer to the chart, and ask the following questions:
  o The number 2 is the double of what number? How do you know?
  o Repeat for numbers 4 to 32?

Task B (Individual, Whole Group):

- Present the following situation to the children:

The McFay's cousins: Judy, Joan, Jane, Jill, Jami and their mom, Mama McFay, decide to go to Minnie's Diner and order cherry pies:

> Judy orders one pie.
>
> Joan wants two more than Judy.
>
> Jane wants two more than Joan.
>
> Jill wants two more than Jane.
>
> Jami wants two more than Jill.
>
> And Mama McFay wants two more than Jami.

- Ask the following questions:
  - Do you predict Mama McFay will get more pies than Papa McFay? Why?
  - How many pies will each person get?
- Allow time for children to find the number of pies for each person.
- Record findings on the group chart.

Judy	Joan	Jane	Jill	Jami	Mama

- Write an equation to show the number of pies each cousin, except Judy, orders.
- Discuss the difference between doubling a number and finding 2 more than a number.

Explore Observations:

- What strategies are used to make predictions?
- What strategies do the children use to find the number of plates of food each brother eats? How many pies Papa eats?
- How do they represent their solution? Can they do it with numbers?
- Can they write equations to show doubling? Adding 2?
- Do children notice the difference between doubling and adding 2?

Consolidate:

Task A (Partners, Whole Group):

- Complete: **How Many Pies?** (Appendix B [10]).
- Discuss solutions with the whole group.

Task B (Individual, Whole Group):

- Pose the following problem to the children:

If Grandpa McFay comes in after Papa McFay and orders a double, how many cherry pies would Minnie have to serve him?

- Make a prediction; check it. Share solutions.
- Write an equation to show how Minnie might know how many pies.

Task C (Partners):

- One child rolls a number cube (1 to 6). The other child says the double.
- Record. Take turns. Children make their own chart. Do for six turns each.

Number	Double

Variation: Give children two cubes. One child rolls both cubes, makes a two-digit number from the numbers showing on the faces of the rolled cubes, and the other child doubles it. Take turns.

Task D (Partners, Whole Group):

- Write the following two scenarios and read together.

Magic Purse A: You have one penny and a magic purse. The purse is magic because when you put your money in the purse it doubles.

Magic Purse B: Its magic works in a different way. When you put your one penny in the purse, it adds two pennies to the amount put in the purse.

- Ask the following question:
  ○ Predict: Which purse would you rather have? Why?
- To check predictions for Purse A drop a penny into the purse, allow it to double, and then take them out. Repeat this six times.
- To check predictions for Purse B drop a penny into the purse, allow it to add two pennies, and then take them out. Repeat this six times.
- Give each child **Double or Add 2** (Appendix B [11]) to keep track of his or her calculations.
- Display a similar group chart to record children's answers. Discuss the patterns in the two columns. Discuss which purse they would rather have and why.

Magic Purse A: The numbers are 2, 4, 8, 16, 32, and 64. Some may notice that each number is found by adding the previous one to itself; others may relate to multiplication and say each number is found by multiplying the previous one by 2. Relate to doubling and twice as much as in the story.

Magic Purse B: The numbers are 3, 5, 7, 9, 11, 13. Each one is 2 more than the previous one, or each number is found by adding 2 to the previous one.

- Share ideas about what is learnt about the difference between doubling and adding 2.

Consolidate Observations:

- How do children double the numbers? Are some using counters?
- How close are predictions for doubling 32?
- Are children surprised by the difference between doubling and adding 2?
- Are the children able to determine the patterns in the two columns in the table? Can they extend to larger numbers?

Extend:

Task A (Individual, Whole Group):

- How does Bill's physical size compare to Will's size? How do you know?
- Phil is twice as big as Will. How much bigger do you think he is than Bill? How do you know?
- Gill is twice as big as Phil? How much bigger is he than Bill? Will? How do you know?
- Children could model sizes of brothers with modeling clay.

Task B (Whole Group):

- Discuss the reality of the following:
  - o Eating that much food as is shown in the story?
  - o Minnie carrying a tray with that much food?

Task C (Whole Group):

- How big do you think Papa McFay is? Why?
- Why do you think John Manders, the illustrator, draws Papa McFay's shadow so big?

Reflection and Discussion:

Children (Individual, Whole Group, Teacher-Posed Questions):

- Did you enjoy or not enjoy the illustrations? What made them enjoyable or not enjoyable?
- What characters did you like or not like? Why?
- Have you ever experienced anything that happened in the story? Tell about it.
- Were there any surprises in the story? If so, what were they?
- Was there anything humorous in the story and/or illustrations for you? What were they? How did the author and/or illustrator make them humorous?

- What did you find most enjoyable about the **Investigation**? Why? Were you surprised by any of your answers?
- What are you still wondering about doubling and twice as much?

Teacher(s) (If possible, share responses with colleagues.):

- Would you recommend *Minnie's Diner: A Multiplying Menu* to your colleagues? Why or why not?
- Was this an enjoyable, successful **Investigation** to implement? If so, what makes it so?
- Did you have to alter your teaching plan during the **Investigation**? If so, why?
- How did your choice of teaching strategies increase the children's opportunities to engage in critical thinking during the **Investigation**?
- What tasks were most effective? Least effective?
- Were there any new strategies the children used in reading and accomplishing the tasks? If so, what were they?
- Were children surprised to what happens to numbers when you add 2 to them compared to when you double them? Did it make sense to them?

EQUAL GROUPS

How Do You Count a Dozen Ducklings?

Sean Chae

Illustrated by Seung Ha Rew

Summary: When Mama Duck's eggs begin to hatch, she counts each one. To her amazement, 12 hatch. She exclaims, "Wow, TWELVE. That's a lot of ducklings!" She wonders how she is going to keep track of them when they go to the pond. Counting them is "too hard." After giving her situation much thought, she decides to group and regroup her ducklings in various ways (e.g., by 2s, 3s, 4s, and finally by 6s). After a number of excursions to the pond, Mama Duck and her ducklings confront a hungry old wolf who is looking desperately for **LUNCH**! What is the best grouping for Mama Duck to group her ducklings to attack the wolf? What do you think is the best grouping to defeat the wolf? Mama Duck knows. An entertaining, engaging story that introduces the mathematical concepts of skip counting, grouping, addition, multiplication, and division. Rew's double-page spreads of bold oil pastels and paint depict fittingly the frolicking, triumphant characters and pondside setting.

INVESTIGATION: THAT'S A LOT OF DUCKLINGS

Mathematics and Literature Experiences

Learning Expectations:

- To divide a number of objects into equal groups—concretely and pictorially—and record the corresponding addition and multiplication equations

- To connect equal groups and repeated addition to multiplication
- To construct viable arguments and critique the reasoning of others
- To use information gained from the illustrations and text to demonstrate understanding of the plot
- To increase ability to think critically
- To learn how visual language communicates ideas and shapes thought and action

Learning Resources: Multiple copies of *How Do You Count a Dozen Ducklings?* and counters

Read Aloud (Whole Group, Teacher as Reader):

- Explore and discuss the book jacket—its title, author, illustrator, and illustration.
- Share and discuss responses to the question posed in the title.
- Read the summary of the story, and discuss why it is provided.
- Share the reviews and why they are provided.
- Read the entire story to enhance literacy skills—for example, vocabulary development, ability to comprehend.
- Allow time to view each double-page spread so that a connection is made between the text and illustration, and greater meaning of the story is gained.
- If a discussion is initiated at the completion of the story, allow time for it.
- Place multiple copies of *How Do You Count a Dozen Ducklings?* in the math center for further examination and rereading.

Engage:

Task A (Whole Group):

Resource: Copies of *How Do You Count a Dozen Ducklings?*

- Reread together the entire story, stopping to relate the text to the illustrations.

  Here are some samples:
  o "One, two, three, four, five, six . . . and there were more. Seven eggs, eight, nine, ten! Eleven! Yikes! And twelve!" Take turns counting the eggs.
  o "Mama saw one, two, three, four. Five, six . . . .uh-oh there were more. Seven ducklings! Eight, nine, ten, eleven! Whew! And twelve." Take turns counting the ducklings.
  o "She sorted her ducklings into short little lines so she counted them two at a time. Now when Mama counted, she only had to count to Six. Six times Two." Count by 2s, bringing attention to how many ducks.

- Ask the following question:
  o What did Mama mean when she said she only had to count to 6? Clarify. Allow time for children to make sense of this statement by expressing their own reasoning about counting by 2s.

(In fact, Mama still counted to 12 but only said 6 numbers: 2, 4, 6, 8, 10, 12.)

- Continue for the different groupings described in the book—"She sorted the ducklings into even longer lines so she could count them six at a time . . . ." Continue to relate content and language to illustrations on corresponding pages.

Engage Observations:

- Can children count the pictures of the 12 eggs and 12 ducklings accurately?
- Do children relate the language used in the book for equal groups to the illustrations?
- Do children understand that counting by 2s (3s, 4s, 6s) to 12 gives the same count as counting by 1s to 12?
- Can children relate the equal groups to the addition equation?
- Can children relate the multiplication equation to the addition of equal groups, the addition equation, and the illustrations?

Explore:

Task A (Whole Group):

- Choose 12 children to be ducklings. Other children sit in a semicircle.
- Together count to check that there are 12 ducklings standing.
- Say, Mama Duck finds it too hard to count each one by ones. She wants to count by 2s.
- Ask the following question:
  o How will the ducklings arrange themselves so it will make it easy to count by 2s?
- Allow time for grouping, than count the ducklings by 2s.
- Ask the following question:
  o How many ducklings? (Some may think there are only 6; take time so all children know that counting by 2s (2, 4, 6, 8, 10, 12) actually gives a final count of 12 objects, even though only 6 numbers are recited.
- Record an addition equation for the equal groups:

$$2 + 2 + 2 + 2 + 2 + 2 = 12$$

- Record as a multiplication equation:

  Say, "6 groups of 2 can be written as 6 x 2 = 12."

Note: *If this notation is new, take time to relate to the addition of equal groups and the corresponding language in the book: "Now the ducklings tottered along two by two. They swam in twos and ate in twos. Six twos! She watched them all, and she kept track: two four, six, eight, ten, twelve!"*

- Repeat for groups of 3, groups of 4, and groups of 6, each time writing the equations and relating the symbols to the language.

Task B (Whole Group):

Note: *The purpose of this* ***Task*** *is to clarify a misconception in the book related to counting the ducks when they are in groups. For example, "Mama . . . decided six was too hard to count! Four would be better . . . . She sorted her ducklings in new little lines so she could count them three at a time. This way, when she counted, she only had to count to FOUR."*

- Have the children do the following:
  - ○ Have 12 children stand in a line and group themselves in 3s.
- Count together: 3, 6, 9, 12.
- Discuss, allowing time to explain why Mama thought she only counted to 4.
- Repeat for other groupings (2s, 4s, 6s) cited in the book.

> ### Explore Observations:
> - Are children able to sort themselves into equal groups?
> - Do children understand that when they sort into different groups that the count (12) does not change? Or do they make the same mistake as the fox?
> - How do they count the equal groups? Can they count by 2s? 3s? 4s? 6s?
> - Do they know that Mama Duck is not correct when she divided the ducks into groups of four and says, "This way, when she counted, she only had to count to three"?

Consolidate:

Task A (Partners, Whole Group):

Center Task

Resources: Equal Groups for 12 (Appendix B [12]) and counters

- Provide partners with a copy of **Equal Groups for 12.** Model with whole group then partners complete at a math center.
- Share and discuss findings with the whole group.
- Ask the following questions:
  - ○ Do you think we found all the equal groupings? Share why you think so.
  - ○ Do you see any patterns in the way the ducklings could be sorted into equal groups?

Task B:

- Repeat **Task A** for different numbers (e.g., 8, 16, 24).

> ### Consolidate Observations:
> - Are the children able to find all the equal groups for 12? Do they go back to the story to find them?
> - Can they write the corresponding addition and multiplication equations?
>
> *(Continued)*

(Continued)

- Do they make the connection between adding equal groups and multiplication?
- When finding the equal groups for 8, 16, and 24, are they persistent in finding all the equal groups or do they give up after finding one or two?
- Do the children work cooperatively to find all the groups?
- Are the children able to write the addition and multiplications equations for groups made from 8, 16, and 24?

Extend:

Task A (Whole Group):

- Mama Duck counts the twelve ducklings and says, "That's a lot of ducklings." What do you think she means? Do you think there is a lot of ducklings? Why or why not?

Task B:

- Read, "The old wolf who lived there . . . was hungry! And what was that smell . . . ducklings! How many? He heard Mama count 'one, two. . . . .' But it was enough for LUNCH!"
- Ask:
  o Why did the wolf think there were only two ducklings?
  o Was he right? Explain why or why not?

Reflection and Discussion:

Children (Individual, Whole Group, Teacher-Posed Questions):

- Do you ever count by 2s, 3s, or 4s? When? Do you count by some other numbers also?
- Why do some people count by 2s, 3s, 4s, etc., rather than 1s?
- Were you surprised that addition and multiplication are related?

Teacher(s) (If possible, share and discuss your responses with colleagues.):

- What strategies did you use to help children having difficulty understand that when you count groups (skip count) that the count is the same as when you count by 1s? Was this a problem for some of your children?
- If you use this **Investigation** again, what changes, if any, would you make? Why?
- What did you like or dislike about the **Investigation**?
- What did you enjoy or not enjoy about *How Do You Count a Dozen Ducklings?*
- Did your children work cooperatively to find all the equal groups for the numbers? If they did not, what strategies would you use to help them work cooperatively?
- Were you bothered by some of the lines in the story that were not correct mathematically, such as, "She sorted the ducklings into even longer lines so she could count them six at a time. This way, when she counted, she only had to count to Two . . . ." Were the children confused by this or did it allow for a "teachable moment"?

Unit III

Operations and Algebraic Thinking

EQUALITY AND EQUATIONS

Balancing Act

Ellen Stoll Walsh

Equal Shmequal

Virginia Kroll

Illustrated by Philomena O'Neill

Summary (*Balancing Act*): A story of friendship, collaboration, and cooperation between two mice and their friends—as well, a story of wonder. This brief but engaging story unfolds when two mice make a teeter-totter. One stands on one end and the other on the opposite end, balancing it. However, before long a salamander joins them and wants a turn. When it steps on one end of the teeter-totter, it's no longer balanced, but to their surprise another salamander appears and steps on the opposite end—balanced, again! The balancing act continues with other friends until one bird appears and the friends are faced with a problem, "How to include the bird and maintain a balanced teeter-totter?" "What would your solutions be?" Walsh, in her usual artistic style—torn paper collage and tempera double-page spreads—depicts clearly the lively characters of the mice and their friends as they experience many "balancing act" escapades.

Summary (*Equal Shmequal*): Through animal characters, the mathematical concept of "equal" is explored meaningfully. As Mouse observes schoolchildren playing tug-of-war, she decides that it would be fun to try the same with her friends. First, she asks Bear to play—Bear on one end of the rope, Mouse on the other. However, when Bear pulls the rope, Mouse goes flying through the air. She realizes quickly that in order to play this game, the teams have to be *equal*. Before time, Bobcat, Wolf, Rabbit, and Box Turtle arrive and want to play. Mouse maintains that the teams have to be *equal*. But before the game is to be played, Box Turtle wants to know, "What does equal mean, anyway?" Mouse explains it means "fair." So, the animals face a dilemma: "How to divide into two equal (fair) teams?" Many solutions are offered; what might they be? What do you think is the best solution? Through familiar animal characters, Kroll explores meaningfully the mathematical concept of equal, while O'Neill's pastel double-spread illustrations depict the playful but expressive moods of the animals as they try to solve the following: "How to make two equal teams?"

INVESTIGATION: WHAT DOES IT MEAN TO BE EQUAL?

Mathematics and Literature Experiences

Learning Expectations:

- To develop an understanding of the equal sign and to understand equality in relation to a balanced scale
- To solve equations written in different formats
- To communicate reasoning to others
- To ask and answer questions with prompting and support about key details in a text
- To name the author and illustrator of a story and define the role of each
- To experience different kinds of texts on the same topic

Learning Resources: Multiple copies of *Balancing Act* and *Equal Shmequal*, pan balance, same size cubes, and dominoes

Read Aloud (Whole Group, Teacher as Reader):

Note: **Read Aloud** Balancing Act *and* Equal Shmequal *before introducing the* **Engage** *stage.*

Balancing Act:

- Explore the book jacket:
  - o Read and discuss the title.
  - o Share experiences of "balancing."
  - o Read the author/illustrator's name.
- Recall other book(s) by Ellen Walsh (e.g., *Mouse Count*). How are they similar or different?
- Read the book jacket flaps (front and back); discuss why a book has such.
- **Read Aloud** the entire story, allowing children to view the illustrations and predict what will happen next, increasing their ability to think critically.

- If a child (children) initiates a discussion related to the **Read Aloud**, provide time for it.
- Place multiple copies of the *Balancing Act* in the math center for further exploration.

Equal Shmequal:

- Read and discuss the title.
  - What does "equal" mean?
  - Why do you think Kroll uses the word shmequal?
  - What does shmequal mean?
  - What do you think the story is about? Why?
- Read and discuss the back cover's (paperback) information; relate it to the title of the book.
- Share biographical information about the author and illustrator.
- **Read Aloud** the entire story, allowing time for the children to view the illustrations and think about the solutions offered and to make comments and/or predictions.
- After the **Read Aloud** is completed, compare *Balancing Act* and *Equal Shmequal.*

Engage:

Balancing Act

- Read together or a child may read, "The mice made a teeter-totter. It was fun to balance." Allow time to view the illustration.
- Discuss the following:
  - What is a teeter-totter? What other names are used for teeter-totter?
  - Share teeter-totter experiences.
- Ask the following questions:
  - What does it mean to balance? Is this teeter-totter balanced? Why or why not?
  - What do they need to do to balance the teeter-totter? (Make the connection to science.)
- Continue reading together the next page, "One mouse on each end," and ask the following questions:
  - Is it balanced now? Why or why not?
  - What would happen if we put another mouse on the left-hand side of the teeter-totter?
- What would we need to do to make it balance?
- On the next page, read together, "But then a salamander wanted a turn."
- Ask the following questions:
  - What happened?
  - Is the teeter-totter balanced now? Why or why not?

- Continue same questioning when the frog arrives and also when the bird arrives.
- Read together, "Whoops! That's not going to work!"
- Ask the following question:
  - Why isn't it going to work?
- On the next page, share what is noticed.
- Ask the following questions:
  - Is there the same number of creatures on each side of the teeter-totter?
  - Why is it unbalanced? Could it be balanced? How? Why?
- Discuss the weight and number of the creatures. Do the creatures on the left-hand side have the same total weight as the bird?
- Ask the following question:
  - What did you learn about balancing from this story? Share responses orally or in writing.

Equal Shmequal

Note: *The word* equal *is used in different ways, and each time the meaning needs to be clarified.*

- Discuss the following:
  - Talk about the game tug-of-war and its rules. Share experiences.
  - Discuss "seesaw" experiences.
- Read together (p. 3), "Some chose teams for a game. 'The two sides have to be equal!' one of them shouted."
- Ask the following questions:
  - Can you share situations when this situation happened to you?
  - What does the following mean: "the two sides have to be equal"?
- Discuss whether there has to be the same number on each side: boys vs. girls, size, etc.
- Continue reading to p. 6: "I forgot the teams have to be equal."
- Ask the following questions:
  - Why aren't they equal? How do you know?
- Read to pp. 8–9. Mouse says, "Everyone can play as long as the teams are equal." and "What does equal mean, anyway?"
- Ask the following question:
  - What does *equal* mean? Record suggestions, including examples that may not be related to the story (e.g., 2 + 2 equals 4). (symbol not introduced until next section (Explore))
- Discuss p. 10. Mouse says, "Equal means fair."
- Continue reading together to p. 17, stopping to share the different situations the animals propose to make the teams fair.
- Discuss p. 17. Bobcat says, "I thought that instead of equal numbers our teams could have equal weights. We could use the seesaw to figure it out."

- Ask the following question:
  - How could the seesaw help? Record suggestions.
- Read p. 18. "What's on one side of the seesaw is equal to what's on the other side . . . You can tell this because it's straight across."
- Discuss *equal,* seesaw balances, and illustrations up to p. 25 that attempt to make the seesaw balance.
- What does the author mean when she says, "It's straight across"?

Engage Observations:

- What is the children's understanding of balance and equal and the relationship between the two?
- Do the children understand it is not only the number of creatures but their weight that must be considered when checking if teeter-totter is balanced?
- Can they make sense of the different meanings of equal used in *Equal Shmequal?*

Explore:

Task A (Whole Group):

Resources: Number cube (1–6), counters (equal weight) or multilink cubes, and pan balance scale

- Children stand in a semicircle around the pan balance.
- Relate pan balance to seesaw and teeter-totter.
- Select two children to roll the number cubes—one for the left-hand side and one for the right-hand side of the balance.
- The first child rolls the number cube and places that many counters on one side of the pan balance scale—for example, 4.

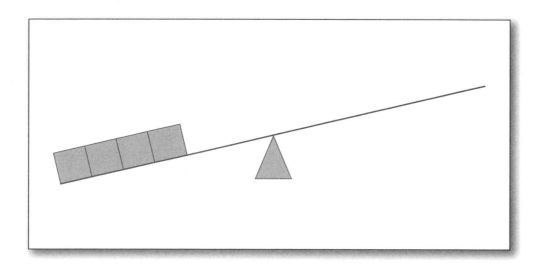

- The second child rolls the number cube and places that many counters on other side of the scale—for example, 6.

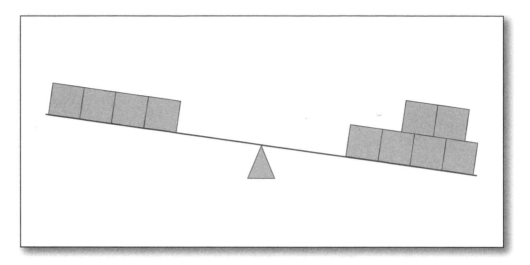

- Ask the following questions:
  - Is the scale balanced? Why or why not?
- Relate to slant of the pan balance and the number of cubes of same size.
- Ask the following questions:
  - How many cubes do we need to add to balance the scales?
  - Which side do we need to place them?
- The first child does it.

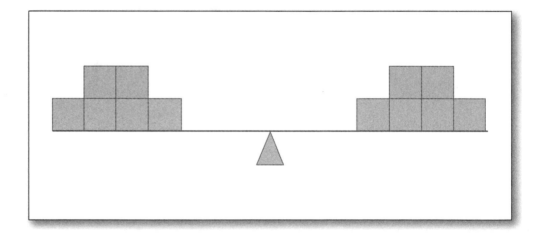

- Ask the following questions:
  - Is it balanced? Why?
- Ask a child to write the equation to represent the balanced scale $(4 + 2 = 6)$.
- Discuss the equation as it relates to adding cubes to the balance.
- Talk about the use of the equals sign.
- Children continue to take turns rolling the cubes, placing counters on the balance and writing equations until there is confidence and fluency in doing same.

Note: *Examples of special cases that may occur:*

- *A 3 is rolled for the left-hand side and a 3 for the right-hand side. Discuss if the scale is balanced. Write the equation 3 = 3. Bring children's attention to this case as an equation.*
- *A 6 is rolled for the left-hand side and a 4 for the right-hand side. Children may suggest to add 2 to the right-hand side.*

Record 6 = 4 +2. It is balanced—same amount on both sides of the equation.

Another might suggest take away 2 from the left-hand side. Record 6 – 2 = 4. It is important that children note the relationship between 6 = 4 +2 and 6 – 2 = 4.

Task B (Individual, Whole Group):

- The first child rolls the number cube and puts that many counters on the left-hand side of the scale (e.g., 2).
- The second child rolls the number cube and puts that many counters on the right-hand side of the scale (e.g., 5).
- As number counters are placed on the scale, record the corresponding numbers so all can see.

Left-Hand Side   Right-Hand Side
2   5

- The first child rolls the cube again and, for example, rolls a 6, places 6 counters on the left-hand side of the balance and the number is recorded along with addition symbol to show the 6 has been added to the left-hand side.

Left-Hand Side   Right-Hand Side
2 + 6   5

- Children suggest how many counters to add to or take away from the pan on the right-hand side to make it balance.
- They agree 3 counters. Add them to the balance and record 3 in the equation; use the addition sign. Since the equation is balanced the = sign can be added.

_____2_____ + _____6_____ = _____5_____ + _____3_____

- Read together, "Two plus six equals five plus three."
- Ask the following question:
  - How do you know both sides are equal? The answer could be as follows: "Because 2 + 6 = 8 and 5 + 3 = 8. Both sides are equal."
- Continue rolling number cubes and balancing the scale until children are confident and fluent in balancing equations.
- Children repeat **Task A** at a math center where there is a balance, number cubes, counters, and a recording sheet.

Explore Observations:

- Do children understand equality in relation to the balance scale?
- Do children understand the meaning of "equals"?
- Are the children able to relate the actions of adding to or taking away cubes from the pan balance scale to the corresponding equation?

Consolidate:

Task A (Partners):

Resource: 20 dominoes (10 pairs of matching ones). Matching means that a pair of dominoes has the same total number of dots.

- The first child turns over two dominoes.

   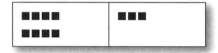

- If partners agree that they match, the second child does the following:
  - Records the equation 6 + 5 = 8 + 3
  - Keeps the two dominoes.
- If the dominoes do not match, they are placed back in the pile of dominoes.
- Partners check each other's work.
- Partners take turns and play continues until all matching dominoes are found.

Task B (Individual):

- Complete **Balance the Equation** (Appendix C [1]) by placing the correct number in the □ to make both sides of the equation equal.

Consolidate Observations:

- What strategies do the children use to match the dominoes?
- Are children fluent in writing the corresponding equation for matching dominoes?
- Can they explain why the two dominoes are equivalent?
- How fluent and confident are they in filling in missing numbers in equations? Are some formats more challenging than others?
- What strategies do they use to find the missing numbers?

Note: *Children are exposed to the equal signs as early as kindergarten in situations like 2 + 2 = 4. However many teachers notice that children view an equation, such as 4 + 3 = □, as telling them to do something, usually add or subtract. Hence, when given 4 + 3 = □ + 2, they often write 7 for the missing number in the box. They see it as find the answer to 4 + 3, write the answer in the box and do not understand they have to* *find equivalent expressions for both sides of the equals sign. Both sides need to balance. Also, when children see □ = 4 + 3 often they do not know what to do and say you can't do it. They need to see equations written in this form, saying what number equals 4 + 3.*

Reflection and Discussion:

Children (Individual, Whole Group, Teacher-Posed Questions):

- What concept do these two books have in common? Explain.
- If your friend asked you what balance means what would you say?
- If your friend asked you what equals means what would you say?
- After doing this **Investigation,** what did you learn about equations that you did not know before?

Teacher(s) (If possible, share and discuss responses with colleagues.):

- Do your children have an understanding of a balanced scale in relation to the equal sign?
- Was this lesson effective in meeting the **Learning Expectations**? In what way?
- What would you do differently in this **Investigation** if using it again?
- What additional assistance or resources would further enhance this lesson?
- What is the greatest challenge for children when they are balancing equations?
- Consider the array of items you have in your classroom. Create a balancing experiment for your children using selected items. Discuss the outcome(s) and why or not why the experiment was successful.

DECOMPOSING NUMBERS/ WORD PROBLEMS

Quack and Count

Keith Baker

Summary: Seven frolicking ducklings take a delightful adventure through a lively marshy terrain where they slip and slide, play peekaboo and water tricks, and even chase busy bumblebees. Through their playful activities, the concepts of addition and equality are explored in an unobtrusive way. In each of Baker's detailed earth tone cut-paper collage illustrations, he presents skillfully the number 7 as the sum of two addends. For instance, in the double-page spread depicting "7 ducklings, 1 plus 6/In the water playing tricks," he illustrates on the left page 1 duckling gleefully standing on a rock, while on the right page, 6 ducklings enjoying being bottom up. Later, in two double-page spreads, 7 ducklings "paddling, flapping, flying" are depicted in three groups. One spread portrays 3 + 2 + 2, and the other spread shows 2 + 3 + 2. Written in rhyming couplets, with repetitive language, this engaging book is predictable but also affords the children many opportunities to make predictions.

INVESTIGATION: HOW MANY DUCKLINGS?
Mathematics and Literature Experiences

Learning Expectations:

- To decompose numbers and write them as the sum of two other numbers in more than one way
- To demonstrate an understanding of equation as balance and the meaning of an equal sign
- To solve word problems with three addends to 20
- To make generalizations and use them to make predictions
- To model with mathematics
- To represent mathematical ideas in multiple ways
- To explore and connect mathematical language in a meaningful context
- To use spoken and written language to communicate mathematical reasoning coherently and effectively to others
- To acquire information and build understanding from poetic text

Learning Resources: Multiple copies of *Quack and Count* and interlocking cubes

Read Aloud (Whole Group, Teacher as Reader):

- Explore and discuss the relationship between the book jacket and book content:
  - Look at the book jacket's illustration. What do you think this book is about? Why? Discuss responses.
  - Read the title. Discuss how the title and the jacket's illustration are related.
  - Read the author's name.
- Read for pleasure *Quack and Count.* Provide time to view each double-page spread.
- If a discussion is initiated after the reading, take time for it.
- Place multiple copies of *Quack and Count* in the math center for independent, peer, or home reading.

Engage:

Task A (Partners, Small Groups, Whole Group):

Resources: Multiple copies of *Quack and Count,* interlocking cubes, and chart paper or whiteboard

- Provide 14 interlocking cubes—7 of one color and 7 of another color to partners—and a copy of *Quack and Count* for each group. Demonstrate the making of a 7-cube train with two different colors.

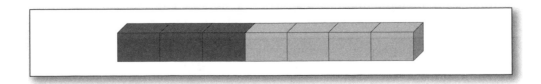

- Ask the following question:
  - How would you describe this 7-cube train? Discuss the number of cubes of each color—that is, 3 red* and 4 green* and that like colored cubes are next to each other.

* *Red cubes appear as black, and green cubes appear as gray in the examples shown.*

- Show an example of a train that does not meet the rules for making a 7-cube train. Discuss and share ideas what is and what is not a 7-cube train.

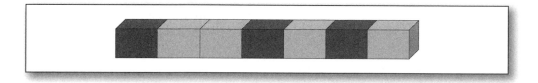

- Partners make a 7-cube train, using as many of each of two colors they wish, but the total is 7.
- Check each other's train to see if the criteria are met.

Continue to make all possible trains with 7 cubes.

Note: *Not all children will find the six 7-cube trains. Many feel the task is completed when they have found one or two trains. When there is an opportunity to share solutions, children will see that there may be more possibilities than the one(s) they found.*

Record the trains made and color cubes, and print the number of cubes used, for example:

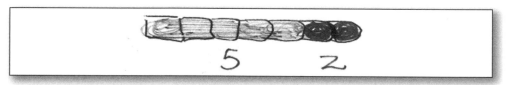

- Share recorded trains with the whole group. Allow time to discuss whether each train meets the criteria and share if anyone has one like it. Continue until all 6 trains are shown.
- Partners say the colors and the numbers representing their train. Record numbers in two columns:

Red	Green
6	1
5	2
4	3
3	4
2	5
1	6

Note: *As children share answers they will not necessarily be in the order shown on the chart. Rearranging in an orderly way helps children note if all possible sums have been found.*

*If 0 addend is suggested (e.g., 7 + 0 or 0 + 7) agree that it is a possible answer, but you might wish to delay including it until you do the **Investigation** based on the book* The Tub People *(Conrad, 1995).*

- When all possibilities are recorded, ask the following question:
  - What did you notice about the trains? Display the previous recording along with the corresponding models or drawings of the trains.

  Here are some sample responses:

  - When there are fewer red cubes, there are more green—for example, when there are 6 red, there is 1 green; when there are 5 red there are 2 green.
  - As red blocks go down by 1, the green blocks go up by 1.
  - As green blocks go up by 1, the red blocks go down by 1.
  - You always have 7 blocks—for example, 6 red and 1 green and 5 red and 2 green.
  - If you add the number in the red column to the number in the green column you get 7.
  - You can have 6 red and 1 green and 1 red and 6 green. They both add to 7 but the trains look different.

Task B (Whole Group):

- Read together the first three or four double-page spreads of *Quack and Count.*
- Ask the following questions:
  - What does "plus" mean? Could the author have said plus in another way?
  - What is the mathematical symbol for plus? Record.
- While reading together, record the equations for different representations of 7 as stated and illustrated by the author, using + instead of plus, starting with $7 = 6 + 1$, $7 = 5 + 2$, $7 = 4 + 3$, etc.
- Refer to recorded equations, and together read each (e.g., 7 is equal to 6 plus 1), relating words to symbols and illustrations.
- Brainstorm the following:
  - What does the = symbol tell us?
  - What is an equation?
  - What do you notice about the recorded equations?

Note: *An equation is like a balance. The expression on the left-hand side of the equality sign is equivalent to the expression on the right-hand side of the equation. If this is the first time that children have written equivalent expressions as equations, allow time to discuss why they are called equations and what they mean. Children must know that the equal sign shows that two expressions have the same value (e.g., the number 7 has the same value as 6 + 1). The equals sign tells us that values on both sides of the equation are the same, even though they are written with different symbols. They also need to know that = signifies equality. The recorded equations (following the storyline in*

the book) may look different to the children and not the familiar 6 + 1 = 7 format.
*Take time to refer to the **Investigation**: Balancing Act (Walsh, 2001) and Equal*
Shmequal (Kroll, 2005). It gives a more in-depth investigation of balancing, equals,
and equations.

Engage Observations:

- How do the children decide how many of each colored cube to use to total 7?
- Do they remember the total must be 7 to keep like colors together?
- What do they do if they repeat a train?
- Are they wondering about "turnarounds," such as 3 + 4 and 4 + 3?
- What encouragement do the children need to find all possible trains?
- Do they make a train using only one color? What do they wonder?
- Do they understand that 7 = 4 + 3 is a symbolic representation of the author's verse "7 is 4 plus 3"?
- Can they represent plus as +?
- Do they understand that = is the symbol for equality?

Explore:

Task A (Partners, Whole Group):

Resource: Interlocking cubes

- Assign a number 5, 8, or 9 to each set of partners.
- Ask the children to do the following:
  - Find all the ways you can represent your number as the sum of two other numbers. Use interlocking cubes.
  - Record all the ways to represent your number, using colored drawings, numbers, and/or equations.
- Make three columns on the whole group recording sheet.
- As different representations for each number are shared, record on the group chart:

5	8	9
4 + 1	7 + 1	8 + 1
3 + 2	6 + 2	7 + 2
2 + 3	5 + 3	6 + 3
1 + 4	4 + 4	5 + 4
	3 + 5	4 + 5
	2 + 6	3 + 6
	1 + 7	2 + 7
		1 + 7

- Ask the following questions:
  - Does writing the sums help you to find all the addends? In what way?
  - What do you notice about the number of ways 5, 8, and 9 can be written as the sum of two addends?
  - If you had to do addends for 4, how many do you predict you would have? Allow time to check the prediction.

Note: *Some children may wonder if 7 = 6 +1 is the same as 1 + 6 = 7. This is an opportunity to discuss that addition is commutative or as some children say turnarounds.*

Task B (Partners):

- Write equations for their findings in **Task A**; then check equations with another set of partners.

Explore Observations:

- Do children use the blocks to find the representations for their number?
- How do they keep track of the sums?
- Do they give up before finding all the sums?
- What strategies do children use to determine they have found all the sums?
- Does listing the sums in order help children figure a strategy to find all the sums?
- Does anyone suggest that 0 could be one of the addends?
- Does anyone notice that the number of ways a number can be decomposed as sum of two addends is one less than the number itself?
- Can they use this generalization to predict how many addends for any other number?
- Do they notice that addition is commutative (the order in which the two addends are added does not affect the sum)?

Consolidate:

Task A (Individual, Partners, Whole Group):

- Predict the number of ways 6 can be written as the sum of two addends and why.
- Ask each child to do the following:
  - Find all the ways 6 can be represented as the sum of two numbers. Use drawings, interlocking cubes, or material of choice to find the two addends. Record equations for the solutions. Check with partner to see if all solutions are found. Compare with predictions made earlier.
  - Design a double-page spread similar to *Quack and Count*, illustrating one of the representations found for 6. Write a rhyming couplet similar to *Quack and Count*. Illustrate.

- o Share double-page spreads. Collect those that represent the same equation—for example, $6 = 1 + 5$. Compile.
- Ask the following question:
  - o What mathematics did you learn by doing this **Task**? Record responses.

Task B (Individual, Partners, Whole Group):

- Repeat the previous **Task** for the number 10.

Consolidate Observations:

- Can they find all the representations of the given number?
- Do they try to find all representations or do they give up when they have found one or two?
- What strategies do they use in designing their page?
- Can they make predictions of number of addends for numbers 6 and 10 based on previous generalization?

Extend:

Task A:

- Revisit the second to last double-page spread in *Quack and Count*. Discuss how the ducklings are arranged (2 on the left, 3 in the middle, 2 on the right). Challenge the children to represent the illustration of ducklings as an equation and record—that is, $7 = 2 + 3 + 2$ or $2 + 3 + 2 = 7$.
- Discuss why these equations are the same.
- Ask the following question:
  - o What other ways do you think the author could group the 7 ducklings in three groups? Use multilinks, cutouts of ducklings, or other material of choice to show the ducklings as three different groups, different from the way the author showed them.
- Make a drawing of one of the ways, and write the corresponding equation.
- Share and record the different equations for writing 7 with three addends.

Note: *12 Ways to Get to 11 **(Merriam, 1993)** is another good resource for representing numbers as the sum of 3 or more addends.*

Task B (Individual):

- Represent 10 as three different numbers. Can you do it in more than one way? Illustrate and write the numbers. Write a rhyming couplet similar to *Quack and Count* and illustrate.
- Numbers from 4 to 20 could be assigned according to children's needs.

Task C:

- Using the shared writing strategy, have the children retell the story of *Quack and Count* from the 3 ladybugs' point of view and illustrate using cut-paper collage technique. Make a big book for read aloud or shared, peer, independent, or home reading.

Reflection and Discussion:

Children (Individual, Whole Group, Teacher-Posed Questions):

- Would you recommend *Quack and Count* to a friend? Why or why not?
- If you were to write to Keith Baker about one thing you would change in *Quack and Count*, what would it be? Why?
- What did you find challenging in the **Investigation**? Did you like that? Why or why not?
- Did listening to the solutions presented by other children help you understand better what you were doing? What did you learn from listening?
- If you had to write the number 25 as the sum of addends, how many different sums do you predict there will be? Why?

Teacher(s) (If possible, discuss responses with colleagues.):

- What did you learn about children's understanding of writing numbers as the sum of two numbers by observing them doing this **Investigation**?
- How is children's sharing of their work beneficial to other children's learning?
- What ways do you have for encouraging children to listen to one another?
- What types of questions or prompts best work for getting children to share their reasoning?
- What if a child wonders why the author had not included $0 + 7$ and $7 + 0$? Some other children responded because it doesn't make sense. How would you discuss these comments with your children?
- "To mathematize is to focus on the mathematical aspects of a situation and then to formulate that situation in mathematical terms; it is a means for children to deepen, extend, elaborate, and refine their thinking as they explore ideas and lines of reasoning" (National Council of Teachers of Mathematics [NCTM], 2010, p. 2). How did this happen in this **Investigation**?

ADDITION WITHIN 20

The Tub People

Pam Conrad

Illustrated by Richard Egielski

Summary: An imaginative fantasy that embeds implicitly the mathematical concept of "how many" that may be explored in multiple ways. The story is about the adventures of seven small, rigid, wooden figures known as the Tub People—father, mother, grandmother, doctor, policeman, child, and dog. Every day they stand in the same order, "in a line . . . on the edge of the bathtub," until it is bath time. That's when the escapades begin—for example, the father playing sea captain rescues the child when he slips off the soap, the policeman and the doctor having water races. However, on one occasion disaster strikes. The Tub People are devastated! The Tub Child falls off the soap and the Tub Father is unable to save him. He is washed down the drain. Fortunately, a plumber comes eventually to the Tub People's aid and retrieves the Tub Child. The Tub People are united happily again. Egielski's realistic watercolor full-page illustrations enhance the story's childlike point of view.

INVESTIGATION: HOW MANY ON THE SIDE OF TUB? HOW MANY ON THE SOAP?

Mathematics and Literature Experiences

Learning Expectations:

- To represent numbers up to 20 as the sum of two addends
- To write equations to show the relationship between three or more numbers
- To use 0 to tell how many in a set with no elements
- To find multiple solutions to a problem and represent solutions in multiple ways
- To look for patterns and make a generalization
- To increase cognitive abilities, including the ability to think critically
- To use spoken and written language to communicate mathematical reasoning coherently and effectively to others
- To provide a model of expressive, fluent reading

Learning Resources: Multiple copies of *The Tub People*; objects to represent the Tub People; and chart paper, whiteboard, or overhead projector

Read Aloud (Whole Group, Teacher as Reader):

- Discuss the title and jacket illustration of *The Tub People* and their relationship to each other and the story.
- Read the author's and the illustrator's names. Talk about their roles.
- Ask the following question:
  o Do you know other books by the author and/or illustrator? Share titles, and give an overview of the book.
- **Read Aloud** the entire story with expression and provide the children the opportunity to connect the story to their lives.
- A discussion, initiated by a child or children, may pursue after the reading. Provide time for it.
- Place multiple copies of *The Tub People* in the math center for independent, peer, and home reading.

Engage

Task A (Small Groups, Whole Group):

- Give each small group a copy of *The Tub People*.
- Each group makes a storyboard representing the tub scene as depicted in The Tub People.
- Children choose objects to represent the seven Tub People and name each one as in the story.

Note: *A storyboard can be drawn on plain paper or cover stock. For this* **Investigation,** *it can be simply a drawing of a tub, a bar of soap, and indication of water in the tub.*

- Read together, "There were seven of them, and they always stood in the same order—the father, the mother, the grandmother, the doctor, the policeman, the child and the dog." Children model on their storyboard the seven people standing on the side of the tub and check to ensure there are exactly seven people standing on the tub. The situation could be modeled at the same time on the overhead or whiteboard.
- Continue to read together, "The father . . . would take the mother . . . for a ride on the floating soap. The others stood on the edge of the tub and waved." Children model with their Tub People the ones on the side of the tub and the ones floating on the soap—that is, 4 on the soap and 3 on the tub.
- Ask the children to do the following:
  o Make a drawing to represent what you modeled, along with numbers, to indicate how many on the side of the tub and how many on the soap. Each group checks another group's drawings.
- Each group shows their drawings to whole group and describes what they drew.

Task B (Small Groups, Whole Group):

- Select a drawing from **Task A.** Ask each group to write an equation to represent the drawing.
- Choose groups to share equations (choose ones that are represented differently).
- Record equations—for example, $4 + 3 = 7$; $3 + 4 = 7$; $7 = 4 + 3$; $7 = 4 + 3$. Discuss.
  o If some write *plus* instead of symbol +, record also.
  o Relate the word with the symbol by asking children to share what they know about + and plus. You can also relate to the word *and*.
- Discuss the different equations relating the numbers and the equals sign in the equation to the actions of the Tub People in the story—for example, here are 7 people in all; 4 are on the soap and 3 are on the side of the tub.
- Discuss the meaning of equation—that is, 7 balances the $4 + 3$; 7 is the same value as $3 + 4$; 7 is another name for 4 and 3.
- Discuss other representations of the same equation.

Engage Observations:

- Are children able to model the situations described in the story?
- Are children able to represent the situation modeled on the storyboards with drawings? Use appropriate numbers?
- Are children able to write equations to represent the situation modeled?
- Can the children tell how the equation represents the Tub People in the story situation?
- Do children know that an equation must show the same value on one side of the equals sign as on the other?
- Do children understand that equations such as $7 = 3 + 4$ and $3 + 4 = 7$ are equivalent?

Explore:

Task A (Partners, Whole Group):

- Ask the following question:
    - How many *different* ways can the seven Tub People be arranged so that some are on the side of the tub and some are in the water?
    - Use storyboards and models of Tub People to find solutions.
    - Record solutions with drawings and numbers.
- Using **The Tub People in Two Places** chart (below), do at least one example together.
- Partners take turns recording numbers on **The Tub People in Two Places** (Appendix C [2]).
- When finished (some may not find all possibilities), share findings and record, for example, the following:

The Tub People in Two Places

Soap	Side of Tub	Total Tub People	Equation
1	6	7	
5	2	7	
2	5	7	
6	1	7	
0	7	7	
7	0	7	
3	4	7	
4	3	7	

- Ask the following questions:
    - Did we find all solutions?
    - How do you know? Discuss.

Note: *To help children know if all solutions are found, you may wish to record the whole group's findings in a more organized way, for example:*

The Tub People in Two Places

Soap	Side of Tub	Total Tub People	Equation
1	6	7	
2	5	7	
3	4	7	
4	3	7	
5	2	7	
6	1	7	
7	0	7	
0	7	7	

- Allow time for partners to complete their charts.

Note about Zero: *Take time to discuss that you can have 7 people on the soap and 0 on the side of the tub or 0 people on the soap and 7 people on the tub. Young children often find 0 confusing. They have very few experiences counting 0 objects or talking about sets with 0 objects, and if they do they are more comfortable saying, "There are no dogs or no stamps" than saying that "there are zero dogs or zero stamps."*

In the Quack and Count **Investigation,** *the set with 0 ducklings was not included. If this is the first time children have an opportunity to note that a set can have 0 objects, take time to discuss.*

Mathematicians refer to the set with no members as the empty or null set. Zero belongs to the set of numbers called the whole numbers, which includes 0 and the natural numbers. Natural numbers are often called the counting numbers—that is, 1, 2, 3 . . . .

Task B (Partners):

- Ask the children to do the following:
  - Write an equation, next to the data, for each row on their chart. Demonstrate an example.

Engage Observations:

- Are they motivated to find all the different addends that make 7, or are they satisfied when they find one or two?
- Do they know that the sum of the groups (those on side of tub and those on soap) must always add to 7?
- How do they keep track of the numbers of people to place in each group?
- Do they recheck to ensure there is a total of 7?

- Do they accept that 0 can be one of the addends of 7?
- What strategies do they use to determine if all solutions have been found?
- Can they explain their reasoning when they think they have found all solutions?
- How comfortable are the children in writing equations to correspond to the data?

Consolidate:

Task A (Partners, Whole Group):

- Choose a different number of Tub People than in the story (e.g., 9).

Note: *If some children are having difficulty in finding all the arrangements for 7 people in **Explore Task A,** assign a smaller number, such as 5.*

- Using a storyboard and number of Tub People assigned, find all the different ways that the people can be arranged on the side of the tub and on the soap. Record the ways with drawings and numbers.
- Record on **The Tub People in Two Places** (Appendix C [2]).
- Share solutions and record as in **Engage Task A.**
- Discuss what they notice about the arrangements and if they think they found all solutions and why.

Task B (Partners):

- Write each arrangement from **Task A** as an equation on recording sheet **The Tub People in Two Places** (Appendix C [2]).

Note: *Tasks A and B can be repeated using numbers up to 20. They do provide practice for basic addition and subtraction facts. Having the children organize their different arrangements in drawings and charts and the accompanying discussion helps further the children's abilities to represent information in multiple ways.*

Task C (Partners, Whole Group):

- Write and illustrate a story about one of your Tub People arrangements. Make a book; include book jacket, title, author and illustrator names, publication date, dedication page, and end pages.
- Share the stories.
- Place the stories in the math center.

Engage Observations:

- Are the children comfortable in finding the parts (addends) for the number assigned and representing them on paper?
- Can they write equations for the different arrangements? Do they relate equations to the arrangements?

(Continued)

(Continued)

- Do they want to find all solutions? Do they show perseverance in trying to find all solutions?
- Can they give reasons for and convince others they have found all solutions?
- Do they include an arrangement with 0 Tub People?
- Do the stories reveal that the children have an understanding of "sense of story"?

Extend:

Task A (Individual, Partners, Whole Group):

- Read together: "The father . . . would take the mother . . . for a ride on the floating soap . . . . Once in a while the child . . . would slide off the soap . . . ."
- Children imagine some of Tub People are on the soap, some are on the side of the tub, and some are in the water (more than the child falls off the soap).
- Brainstorm three or four different arrangements of Tub People and record on **The Tub People in Three Places** (Appendix C [3]).

Tub People in Three Places

Number of People on the Side of the Tub	Number of People on the Soap	Number of People in the Water	Total Number of People	Equation

- Partners fill in the numbers on **The Tub People in Three Places** corresponding to the arrangement shown on group recording. Partners continue to find at least 10 arrangements and record on their chart.
- Record all arrangements found on the whole group recording sheet.
- Discuss if all arrangements have been found and how they may know.

Note: *There are several different ways to write 7 as the sum of three addends.*

Task B (Partners, Whole Group):

- Write equations for five of your arrangements from **Task A.**
- Ask the following question:
  - How do you know they are equations? Relate equations to the physical arrangement or drawings.

Task C:

- Repeat **Tasks A** and **B** for a different number of Tub People.

Task D (Small Groups):

- Select one of the arrangements from **Task A,** and write a short play. Dramatize.

Reflections and Discussion:

Children (Individual, Small and Whole Groups, Teacher-Posed Questions):

- What did you find most challenging when finding all the ways to arrange the 7 people?
- Were you surprised when you could have 0 people in one of the groups? Share your thoughts.
- Share what you know about equations.

Teacher(s) (If possible, share and discuss responses with colleagues.):

- What observations did you make when you **Read Aloud** The Tub People? Why?
- How long did you allow your children to wrestle with finding the solution to a problem (e.g., all the ways to arrange 7 people) before you offered help? Do you give hints or ask questions to get them thinking more deeply? If so, share some hints and/or questions.
- What challenges did you face in motivating all the children to find the solutions to a problem?
- What changes might you make to your instructional strategies so that more children will be motivated to find all solutions to a task?
- Share your children's understanding of 0 as a number?

SUBTRACTION WITHIN 20/ WORD PROBLEMS

What's the Difference? An Endangered Animal Subtraction Story

Suzanne Slade

Illustrated by Joan Waters

Summary: An informational book that focuses on 12 land and water endangered animals, such as bald eagles, bowhead whales, red wolves, and gray bats. Each watercolor double-page spread focuses on one threatened animal and includes a text box providing various information about the animal—for example, when the species became threatened, the habitat dangers, and how the situation has improved. From the information and illustration, Slade composes a simple rhyme that invites children to solve a subtraction problem. In addition, there is a section in the back of the book titled "For Creative Minds," which includes such topics as "Endangered Animal Vocabulary," "Food Chains & Webs," and "Fact Families."

INVESTIGATION: HOW MANY IN THE NEST?

Mathematics and Literature Experiences

Learning Expectations:

- To use subtraction within 20 to solve word problems involving taking from, taking apart, and comparing, with unknowns in all positions, by using objects, drawings, and equations with a symbol for the unknown number to represent the problem
- To understand subtraction as an unknown addend problem
- To understand addition and subtraction as inverse operations
- To make sense of problems and persevere in solving them
- To ask and answer questions about key details in a text
- To read prose and poetry of appropriate complexity with prompting and support
- To apply various comprehension and interpretative strategies to informational text

Learning Resources: Multiple copies of *What's the Difference? An Endangered Animal Subtraction Story* and counters

Read Aloud (Whole Group, Teacher as Reader):

- Discuss the book jacket—its title, author, illustrator, and illustration.
- Define and discuss the word *endangered* and what creatures are endangered.
- Ask the following questions:
  o Are there other books you know about endangered creatures?
  o What are the titles?
  o What creatures are endangered?
- Read and discuss the title page information.
- **Read Aloud** the entire text to spark children's interest in the topic and to increase their ability to think critically.

Note: *This book may be **Read Aloud** in different ways. For the purpose of this **Investigation**, one may only **Read Aloud** the simple rhymes. However, one may also **Read Aloud** the information in the text boxes and the rhymes.*

Engage:

Task A (Individual, Whole Group, Teacher):

- Revisit the first double-page spread with eaglets, and read together the rhyme.

- Ask the following questions:
  - How many in the nest? How do you know?
  - Does anyone think differently? Why?
  - The author has 3 − 2 = ? on the left-hand page. How does this relate to the rhyme?
  - How do you read the equation (3 − 2 = ?)?
- Read 3 − 2 = ? semantically: There were 3 eaglets, and 2 fly away. How many are in the nest? Point out that the question mark refers to "how many are in the nest." Read symbolically 3 minus 2 equals how many?
- Reread the rhyme, but use larger numbers (e.g., 9). Together, write the equation and find the answer.
- Repeat for one or two other rhymes.

Note: *Suggest that children say subtract or minus instead of take away for the "−" sign, as later we will be using the same sign to indicate a meaning of subtraction other than take away. Children may be more familiar with □ as a placeholder than ? so take time to clarify.*

Engage Observations:

- How do children find the answer to how many in the nest? Do you think they could have done it the same way if the numbers were larger?
- Do children listen and question the strategies used by others to find the answer?
- Could they relate the equation (3 − 2 = ?) to the words of the rhyme?
- What strategies do they use to find the solution when larger numbers are used?
- Could they write the equation?

Explore:

Task A (Partners, Whole Group):

- Choose a rhyme. Referring to the corresponding subtraction equation on the left-hand page, write a new rhyme to match the equation. Follow the format used by the author; it must be a word problem written as a rhyme. Model the writing of one rhyme with the whole group.
- Partners write one together. Exchange rhymes with another set of partners; solve each other's problem rhymes.
- Select rhymes to share with whole group.

Task B (Partners, Whole Group):

Comparison Word Problems

Resources: Copies of *What's the Difference? An Endangered Animal Subtraction Story* and counters

- Read together the rhyme about the gray bats and matching equation 9 - 6 = ?.

- Present the following word problem:

  In one cave there are 9 bats snoozing.

  Out flying around are 6 bats.

  How many more bats are snoozing than flying?

- Partners record their solution using concrete objects, drawings, words, and an equation.
- Share and discuss selected solutions with the whole group.
- Record all equations presented and compare, such as, 6 + _____ = 9; _____ + 6 = 9; and 9 − 6 = _____ . Discuss how each equation relates to the numbers in the problem and in all cases the answer to the problem is 3 bats.

Task C (Individual, Whole Group):

- Reread the rhyme about the crocodiles:

  In the marsh there were 8 crocodiles.

  Some swam away.

  Now there are 5.

  How many swam away?

- Use concrete objects, drawings, words, and equations to find the solution to the problem. Try to write an equation that is different from the one the author wrote.
- Allow time to find a solution. Record, share, and discuss solutions with the whole group.
- Record all equations.

    Example: One child wrote 8 − ? = 5.

- Ask the following question:

  o How does this equation make sense for finding a solution to the problem?

  The child may say, "8 is the 8 crocodiles and ? is for the number that swam away. The number of crocodiles left is 5."

- Ask the following question:

  o How did you find how many swam away?

  Here are some sample responses:

  o I said how many do you take from 8 to get 5. I counted backwards and got 3. I kept count on my fingers.
  o I counted up from 5 to get 8. I got 3 (showing it with the counters).
  o I used the equation 5 + ? = 8, because I was thinking what do I have to add to 5 to get 8, the number that swam away. Then I counted up.
  o I subtracted 5 from 8 to get the answer so the equation was really 8 − 5 = 3 (verifies with the counters).
  o Note it is also the equation that the author wrote for the solution.

- Record the three equivalent equations children may have suggested for the solution:

  $8 - ? = 5$; $5 + ? = 8$; $8 - 5 = ?$ and relate each equation to the words and numbers in the problem.

Explore Observations:

- What strategies do they use to write a rhyming word problem to match a given equation?
- Do they write a question that was answerable by the information they wrote?
- What strategies and supports do they use to solve the comparison problem?
- Were they confused that the comparison problem was subtraction?
- Can they relate the equation to the problem?
- For the missing addend type problem (change unknown) did they need to use counters to find a solution?
- Were they able to write an equation to correspond to their solution strategy?

Consolidate:

Task A (Partners, Whole Group):

Resource: Endangered Animal Problems (Appendix C [4])

- Copy the word problems, and give them to partners to solve.
- They may be distributed over a period of time.
- Children record solutions to include drawings, words, numbers, and equation.
- Solutions are shared and discussed with the whole group.

Note: *Different types of problems (take away, comparison, missing addend) increase children's understanding of the inverse relationship between addition and subtraction.*

Consolidate Observations:

- What strategies do the children use to find solutions to the problems?
- Are there some problem types (take away, compare, change unknown, how many more, and missing addends) they find more challenging than others? In what way?
- Does using concrete objects help them solve the problems?
- Are they able to record their solutions with drawings, words, numbers, and equations?
- Can they describe to others how they solved a problem?
- Are they listening to solutions presented by others? Do they ask questions to help understand better?

Extend:

Task A:

- Assign previous problems from Appendix C(4) using larger numbers

Task B (Individual, Partners, Whole Group):

- Return to Fact Families (in the back section of *What's the Difference? An Endangered Animal Subtraction Story*).
- With the whole group take each fact family (triangle), and write the equations associated with the three numbers. Do not include the names of the animals.

    Example: For the numbers 4, 2, and 6, record together the following:

    $4 + ? = 6$

    $2 + 4 = ?$

    $6 - 4 = ?$

    $? - 2 = 4$

- Each child copies and provides the answer for each question mark. Check answers with partner.
- Partners write the equations for the other fact families illustrated. Give the answers, and check them with another set of partners.

Task C (Partners, Whole Group):

- Children draw a triangle similar to the one in the book. Everyone writes the number 13 on one of the vertices.
- Partners decide the other two numbers but must be such that they will form a fact family with a sum of 13.
- Share the numbers they used—for example, 12 and 1; 11 and 2; 10 and 3; 9 and 4; 8 and 5; 7 and 6. Discuss why there are so many choices.
- Write the fact families for the numbers they wrote. Partners check each other's work.
- Repeat, but one number must be 11.
- Repeat, but one number must be 14.
- Repeat, but one number must be 10.

Task D (Small Groups, Whole Group):

- Surf the web to identify endangered creature(s) in your state or province.
- List the creature(s).
- Record the following:
    - o Locations where creature(s) live
    - o Habitat(s) of the creature(s)
    - o Reasons why the creature(s) is/are endangered
    - o What action is been taken to prevent further endangerment
    - o A photo or drawing of the creature(s) (if possible)
    - o Website(s) for further information

- Find books of various genres about the creature(s).
- Present and display information.

Reflection and Discussion:

Children (Individual, Whole Group, Teacher-Posed Questions):

- Did you find any of the **Tasks** challenging? Which one(s)? Why?
- What **Task** did you like the best? Why?
- Were you surprised at all the different situations that require subtraction?
- Do you have some special strategies for solving word problems?
- Do you have some special strategies for remembering subtraction facts?

Teacher(s) (If possible, share and discuss responses with colleagues.):

- What was the greatest challenge in implementing this **Investigation** with your children?
- What strategies did you use to help children solve the word problems?
- Often it is said that explaining or showing the children "how" is a more efficient way of getting children to learn mathematical concepts than taking instructional time to discuss their solutions. What do you consider are the advantages and disadvantages of both approaches?
- What challenges are presented in getting children to see that a subtraction equation can represent several different situations (e.g., take away, comparison, how many more?)?
- What suggestions do you have for other teachers using this **Investigation**?

WORD PROBLEMS WITH TWO OR MORE ADDENDS

The Twelve Days of Summer

Jan Andrews

Illustrated by Susan Rennick Joliffe

Summary: *The Twelve Days of Summer* follows the same language pattern as the familiar song "The Twelve Days of Christmas"—for example, "On the first day of summer a child finds A song sparrow nest; On the second day . . . , Two goastsbeard seeds . . . and On the twelfth . . . , Twelve eggs a-hatching." Each new day, a different wonder of nature is discovered and added concretely, pictorially, and symbolically to the previous discoveries. The double-page colorful illustration for each day is full of details—as well as being humorous. Appended is a list of "common and curious" facts about the creatures and plants featured. This engaging poem not only celebrates many creatures found in nature during the summer but also the cycle of life. As well it provides many opportunities to use addition strategies to find sums.

INVESTIGATION: ADDING USING OWN STRATEGIES
Mathematics and Literature Experiences

Learning Expectations:

- To demonstrate an understanding of addition of numbers concretely, pictorially, and symbolically
- To describe and use personal strategies to find the sum of two or more addends
- To solve word problems involving addition
- To communicate mathematical ideas and reasoning to others using appropriate everyday and mathematical language
- To relate the illustrations to the text

Learning Resources: Multiple copies of *The Twelve Days of Summer*, storyboard, and circular counters

Read Aloud (Whole Group, Teacher as Reader):

- Explore and discuss the different book jacket features of *The Twelve Days of Summer*—for example, title, book jacket, end pages, author, illustrator, and their relationship to the story.
- Take time to view and discuss the first double-page spread (no words included). Invite a child to describe it.
- Read aloud the entire book for enjoyment, providing time to explore each illustration and locate the specific wonder of nature featured.
- Place multiple copies of *The Twelve Days of Summer* in the math center for independent, partner, and home reading.

Engage:

Task A (Individual, Partners, Whole Group):

- Before involving the children in the following **Task,** revisit each double-page illustration, locate the specific wonder of nature introduced, and discuss what it is and its specific characteristics (e.g., goatsbeard seeds).
- Provide partners with counters to keep count of the number of gifts received daily and a recording sheet: **Number of Gifts** (Appendix C [5]). Display a whole group recording sheet: **Number of Gifts.**
- Read together the double-page illustration, "On the first day of summer . . . "
- Ask the following questions:
  - o What does the sunshine bring on the first day of summer?
  - o How many? Allow time for responses, bringing attention to the one nest even though the nest has three eggs.
  - o Using the recording sheet, record responses.
  - o Discuss numbers recorded and relate to story.
  - o Allow time for children to find the gift in the illustration.
- Read together the double-page spread, "On my second day of summer . . . ."

- Ask the following question:
  - o What gifts did the sunshine bring?

Note: *Discuss the new gift (two goatsbeard seeds), and repeat the first day gift (a song sparrow nest). This may be confusing for some children.*

- Ask the following question:
  - o How many gifts are received altogether on the second day? Record in the second and third columns in the table. Discuss and relate to the story.
- Continue to read together, and ask the same questions for the third and fourth days. Counters are available if needed to find the total number of gifts each day.

Number of Gifts

Day	Number of Gifts Received Each Day	Total for Each Day
1st	1	1
2nd	2 + 1	3
3rd	3 + 2 + 1	6
4th	4 + 3 + 2 + 1	10
5th		
.		
.		
12th		

- Discuss the completed part of the recording sheet, as follows:
  - o How numbers in the third column (Total for Each Day) relate to the story
  - o Strategies used to find totals in the third column
  - o Patterns noticed in the columns

Possible strategies and patterns:

  - o I used counters (or tallies, fingers) to find the total in Column 3.
  - o We added the number of the day to the number of gifts received the day before.
  - o The numbers in the third column are 1, 3, 6, 10. The pattern doesn't increase by the same number but increases by 2, 3, 4 . . . . So the total on the fifth day will be 5 more or 15;
  - o The number in the third column increases by the same number as the day, etc.

Engage Observations:

- Do children understand the meaning of the words *first, second,* etc.?
- How do children find the total gifts received on a particular day? Do they use counters, fingers, or tallies; add mentally; use paper–pencil; group numbers together; or use patterns?
- Can children connect numbers in the table to the story?
- What observations do the children make when they examine the third and fourth columns of the table?
- Are they able to describe any patterns in the third column? Do they use these patterns to find the total number of gifts?

Explore:

Task A (Partners, Whole Group):

Note: *This **Task** is a continuation of **Engage** in **Task A**. Children need a copy of the* **Number of Gifts** (Appendix C [5]).

- Read together, "On my fifth day of summer . . . "
- Ask children to predict the total number of gifts received on the fifth day. Discuss how the predictions were made.
- Partners check predictions. Share how they found the total number of gifts for the fifth day and how it compares to prediction.
- Fill in the information for the fifth day, and discuss if the patterns they noted for the second, third, and fourth day is still true.
- Partners complete the chart to the twelfth day.
- Record solutions on a whole group recording sheet and discuss strategies used to find solutions and accuracy of totals.

Task B (Individual, Whole Group):

- Refer to the whole group chart for first twelve days.
- Ask the following question:
  o What patterns do you notice?
- Allow time to describe patterns they see and how they know.
- Ask the following questions:
  o If the sunshine continued to bring gifts, can you predict how many gifts there would be on the thirteenth day?
  o What do you predict? How did you make your prediction?
  o How would you check?
- Share solutions and justifications.

Explore Observations:

- What strategies are the children using to add the sequence of numbers for each day?
- What patterns do they notice?
- Do they use the patterns to find the total number of gifts?
- Can they use the patterns to predict the number of gifts for the thirteenth day?
- Can they justify their prediction?
- Is their prediction correct? How do they check?
- Is their addition of numbers accurate?

Consolidate:

Task A (Partners, Whole Group):

Partners solve the following problems:

A. Read together, "On the second day . . . two goatsbread seeds."

She also brought 2 goatsbeard seeds on day 3, 4, 5, 6, 7, 8, 9, 10, 11, 12.

How many seeds does she bring in total if she brings 2 for each of the days?

Find a solution and discuss different strategies used to find it.

B. Read together, "On the third day . . . three ruffed grouse."

She also brought 3 ruffed grouse on Days 4, 5, 6, 7, 8, 9, 10, 11, 12.

How many grouse does she bring in total if she brings 3 for each of the days?

Share and discuss the solution and how it was solved.

C. Read together, Read together, "On the fifth day . . . five bumble bees."

She also brought 5 bumble bees on Days 6, 7, 8, 9, 10, 11, 12.

How many bees does she bring in total if she brings 5 for each of the days?

Share and discuss solutions and how it was solved.

D. Read together, "On the tenth day . . . ten crows a-cawing."

She also brought 10 crows a-cawing on Days 11, 12.

How many crows a-cawing does she bring in total if she brings 10 for each day?

Find a solution, and discuss different strategies used to find it.

Task B (Individual, Partners):

- Each child chooses a double-page spread and writes a problem similar to ones in **Task A.**
- Ask partner to solve.

Consolidate Observations:

- What strategies do the children use to find the solution to the first problem?
- Do they add the numbers or do they count by 2s?
- Do they have trouble keeping track of how many 2s?
- What strategies are they using to add the numbers in the following problems?
- Can they write their own problem? Is it one that has sufficient information for their partner to solve?

Extend (Individual, Whole Group):

- Assume the sunshine brought gifts on the thirteenth day. Write and illustrate a double-page spread for the thirteenth day. Display.
- Find other *The Twelve Days of . . .* books. Share them. Compare the language patterns. As a whole group, using the shared writing strategy with teacher as scribe, create a *Twelve Days of . . .* book, include the main format features of a book (i.e., title, authors' names). Place in the math or reading center for future reading by individuals or partners.

Reflection and Discussion:

Children (Individual, Whole Group, Teacher-Posed Questions):

- What **Task** did you like the best? Why?
- Are you amazed at any of your answers? Why?
- Have you read books similar to this one? What are the titles? What are the books about?

Teacher(s) (If possible, discuss responses with colleagues.):

- Are the **Tasks** at the different stages of this **Investigation** suitable for helping children meet the stated **Learning Expectations**?
- Does sharing and discussing solutions contribute to children's learning of the expectations?
- Do children use patterns and skip counting to find solutions to the word problems?

Unit IV

Operations Within 100 and Place Value

REPRESENTING NUMBERS TO 100/ ADDITION AND SUBTRACTION

One Is a Snail, Ten Is a Crab: A Counting By Feet Book

April Pulley Sayre and Jeff Sayre

Illustrated by Randy Cecil

Summary: Have you ever counted by feet? Well, follow the sign "To The Beach" in *One Is a Snail, Ten Is a Crab: A Counting By Feet Book,* and have fun counting the number of feet a snail, a crab, an insect, a spider, and other creatures have. Find out how many feet 10 people and a crab have altogether or what combination of creatures would be needed to count 90 feet or even 100 feet. Cecil's appealing, rich oil double-page illustrations portray summertime at the beach and its visiting creatures. Throughout this mirthful number book (1–100), he infuses gentle humor by depicting poppy-eyed, jovial, yet sometimes bewildered-looking creatures to describe various number combinations. This number book invites children to count by ones, as well as add and multiply to find the number of feet.

INVESTIGATION: COUNT BY FEET
Mathematics and Literature Experiences

Learning Expectations:

- To represent and describe numbers to 100 concretely, pictorially, and symbolically using base ten and place value
- To decompose numbers
- To add two or more one- and two-digit numbers to get a given number
- To use spoken and written language to communicate mathematical reasoning coherently and effectively to others
- To read a wide range of literary genres to acquire information and build understanding, and for personal fulfillment

Learning Resources: Multiple copies of *One Is a Snail, Ten Is a Crab;* base ten blocks; and number cubes

Read Aloud (Whole Group, Teacher as Reader):

- Introduce the book through its book jacket (title, authors, and illustrator), and also make reference to the end pages, copyright–dedication page, and title page.
- Read for pleasure the entire book *One Is a Snail, Ten Is a Crab* to heighten the children's interest.
- Place multiple copies of *One Is a Snail, Ten Is a Crab* in the math center for independent, peer, and home reading.

Engage (Small Groups, Whole Group, Teacher):

Resources: Multiple copies of *One Is a Snail, Ten Is a Crab;* cubes; and base ten blocks

- In small groups, give each group a copy of the book and open to "30 is three crabs."
- Ask the following question:
  - Why do the authors say, "30 is three crabs"? Children use drawings, equations, cubes, or base ten blocks to show why.
- Select children to share their reasons, and ask the following questions:
  - Why is your answer the same as the number 30?
  - Do you agree with what (child's name) said? Why or why not?
  - Does anyone think differently about this? Tell us.
  - Someone explain why (child's name) is thinking about it that way?
  - Help us understand what he or she said? Show us with the blocks.
  - Does this group have a question?
  - Does it make more sense now? In what way?
- Read together, "Or ten people and a crab," and ask the following questions:
  - Why do you think the authors say this? Allow time for children to suggest why.

o Could the authors have written something different for "ten people and a crab"? Children find a substitute for "ten people and a crab," share solutions, and tell why they make sense.
o Could the authors have shown 30 using only insects? Show how you know. Share solutions.
o Could they have used different creatures to represent 30? If so, what creatures and why. Share solutions.

Engage Observations:

- Are children able to associate the number 10 with a crab?
- How do they calculate 30 using 3 crabs with 10 feet? Do they need to use objects? Count by 10s? Add 10 + 10 + 10? Multiply 3 tens are 30? Use place value?
- Can they write number sentences to show three crabs are 30 (and later for 10 people and a crab)?
- How do they calculate the number of feet for 10 people and a crab?
- What strategies do they use to find different representations for 30?

Explore (Small Groups, Whole Group, Teacher as Guide):

- Read together "70 is seven crabs or ten insects and a crab."
- Discuss the format of the double-page spread, representing 70—that is, an "OR" statement depicted by an illustration representing each part of the statement. Ask the following question:
  o Why did the authors describe 70 in this way?
  o Create a page for 70 similar to the format used in the book, using different creatures (e.g., starfish, birds, octopus). Each illustration of the creatures should clearly show the feet used to make 70.
  o Record on chart paper the statements.

    Seventy is _____ or _____.

  o Have children copy this sentence and complete to represent their illustration. Then write a number sentence to show why their illustration makes sense. Use words and numbers to explain their solution.

Example: If a group says, "Seventy is 10 insects and 10 snails or 5 spiders and 4 crabs," they may write the following:

$70 = 6 + 6 + 6 \ldots$ (10 times) and $1 + 1 + 1 \ldots$ (10 times) or

$70 = 6 + 6 + 6 \ldots$ (5 times) and $10 + 10 + 10 + 10$.

Some may be able to write the sentences above using multiplication symbols, such as follows:

$70 = (10 \times 6)$ and (10×1) or $70 = (5 \times 6)$ and (4×10)

- Groups share their number sentences with the whole group and tell why their representations make sense.

- Ask the following questions:
  - o Did anyone do it the same way? Tell us about it.
  - o Did anyone do it another way? Show us how you did it.
- Record all the number sentences and ask the following questions:
  - o Did we find all the ways to represent 70? How do you know?
  - o Choose another double-page spread between 40 and 90, repeat the previously given **Task.** Display each group's work.

Explore Observations:

- What strategies do they use to represent the number 70?
- Do they use concrete materials or just work with the symbols?
- How accurate are they with their calculations?
- Do they share the reasons for their choice of creatures?
- How do they keep track of the creature's feet to get the target number?
- What strategies do they use for combining the number of feet?
- What methods and tools do they use to compute?
- Do they need support from you and their peers?
- Do they check the reasonableness of their answers?
- Are they eager to find more than one solution to a problem?
- Are all children ready to write mathematical sentences to represent their illustrations?
- Do the children work well together to find solutions?
- Can children show that all possible answers are found for representing 70 using the feet of the creatures in the book?

Consolidate (Individual, Partners):

- Each child chooses a number between 30 and 99 (one not already illustrated in *One Is a Snail, Ten Is a Crab*), records the number and designs a double-page spread to show the number, similar to pages in the book.
- When completed, exchange page with a partner. The partner then writes the number sentence for the illustration. Partners check each other's work.
- Children are challenged to find at least one other way to represent their number. They could find as many as they can and record them.
- Children choose one of their representations (double-page spread) for display.

Consolidate Observations:

- Observations are similar to **Explore Observations** but more emphasis on observations of children working independently.

Extend:

Task A Writing Feet Problems (Individual, Whole Group):

- Share two or three problems with the group, then children create their own feet problems, using creatures of their own choice or ideas from suggested books about animals, insects, etc.

Example 1: I have 2 creatures. The total number of feet is 10. What creatures might I have?

Example 2: I have 8 creatures. The total number of feet is 38. Seven of them are dogs. What might the other creature be?

Example 3: I have 6 creatures. The total number of feet is 29. Four of them are insects. What might the other creatures be?

Note: *Share the solutions. Ask, "Does anyone have a different a solution to share?"*

- Children write similar problems and share with the group.

Task B (Individual, Small Groups):

- Read Eric Carle's, *A House for Hermit Crab* to find out about the hermit crab's habitat. Research other books about crabs. Choose one, identify its type, and describe its habitat. Share with peers.
- There are many different types of crabs. Find books about crabs and identify the type of crab the illustrator depicts in *One Is a Snail, Ten Is a Crab.* Is it a real crab, or is it a fictional one the illustrator imaged? How do you know? Make a book display of the books found.

Task C (Teacher, Small Groups, Whole Group):

- Find other books authored by April Pulley and Jeff Sayre. Find other books illustrated by Randy Cecil. In small groups, children select one of the books and give a short book talk. Display all books for independent, peer, or home reading.
- Search the Internet to find information about the authors and illustrator and design an authors' and/or illustrator's website to display with the book display.

Reflection and Discussion:

Children (Individual, Whole Group, Teacher-Posed Questions):

- What did you like most about doing this **Investigation**?
- Did you find any of the tasks challenging? In what way?
- Do you think you found all possible ways to make your number? Why or why not?

Teacher(s) (If possible, share and discuss with colleagues.):

- What was the greatest challenge in implementing this **Investigation** with your children?
- What strategies did you use to help children persevere at the tasks in the **Investigation,** especially when children seemed to be struggling?
- One purpose in doing the **Investigation** is to build a "community of discourse" as described in Chapter 2 of this book. How do you evaluate the discourse associated with this **Investigation**?
- Often it is said that explaining or showing the children how is a more efficient way of getting children to learn mathematical concepts than taking instructional time to discuss their solutions. What do you consider are the advantages and disadvantages of both approaches?
- "To improve their mathematics instruction, teachers must constantly analyze what they and their students are doing and how that approach is affecting what the students are learning" (National Council of Teachers of Mathematics [NCTM], 2007, p. 62). How does this statement apply to your practice?

ADDITION AND SUBTRACTION WITHIN 100/WORD PROBLEMS

Centipede's 100 Shoes

Tony Ross

Summary: After hurting one of his toes, a young centipede's mom decides he needs shoes. At the shoe store, he asks for 100 shoes—50 left ones, 50 right ones—since centipede means 100 feet. But does he need 100 shoes? After purchasing 100 shoes (50 pairs), little centipede begins to put them on. However, to his surprise, he has 58 shoes left over! But why? His granddad comes to his rescue, explaining that "most centipedes have only forty-two legs." The centipede is faced with a dilemma: "What to do with the left over shoes?" He decides to share the extra shoes with his friends. But will he get rid of all his shoes? How will he manage to solve his predicament? Using pen-and-ink illustrations, Ross brings humor to this amusing tale, while addition and subtraction skills assist in solving the young centipede's problem.

INVESTIGATION: WHAT DO YOU DO WITH TOO MANY SHOES?

Mathematics and Literature Experiences

Learning Expectations:

- To use addition and subtraction within 100 to solve one- and two-step word problems involving situations of adding to, taking from, putting together, taking apart, and comparing, with unknowns in all positions— for example, by using drawings and equations with a symbol for the unknown number to represent the problem

- To communicate reasoning to others
- To actively engage in group reading with purpose and understanding
- To ask and answer questions about key details in a text
- To apply strategies to comprehend and interpret text

Learning Resources: Multiple copies of *Centipede's 100 Shoes*, counters, linking cubes, and base ten blocks

Read Aloud (Whole Group, Teacher as Reader):

- Discuss the book jacket—its title, author–illustrator, and illustration.
- Make predictions about what the story may be about and why.
- Read the front book jacket flap, and respond to the questions posed.
- Read the entire story to discover and experience the delight in the story.
- Enjoy the story for its content, language, and power to ignite the children's imaginations without questioning.
- Place multiple copies of *Centipede's 100 Shoes* in the math center for independent, peer, and home reading.

Engage:

Task A (Individual, Whole Group):

- Read together, "'One hundred shoes, please! . . . because I'm a centipede, which means a hundred feet,' said the little centipede."
- Discuss the meaning of *centipede.*
- Ask the following questions:

  o Do you know other words that begin with *cent?* List them.
  o Does anyone know the meaning of the word *cent?*
  o If possible, search the web, books, etc., at home, to find the number of feet a centipede has. Discuss and share findings with family. Share with schoolmates.

Note: *The information about centipedes will be helpful with solving and composing word problems in this* **Investigation.** *Centipedes can have many different pairs of legs. The number of pairs is always an odd number.*

Task B (Partners, Whole Group):

- Read together, "He had fifty-eight shoes left over. 'That's because most centipedes have only forty-two legs,' said his granddad."
- Ask the following question:

  o If the grandfather did not tell you the centipede had 42 legs, how could you figure it out?
  o Review what you know:
    □ The centipede has 58 shoes left over.
    □ The centipede buys 100 shoes.
  o Write an equation to show there were 58 shoes left over.
  o Share solutions with a partner, then present to the whole group and explain reasoning.

Note: *Some children may suggest counting the legs in the illustration. Agree that is one way but they must also show it using mathematical notation. Record equations; allow time for children to explain and justify how their equation is used to find a solution. Some children may write $100 - 58 = 42$; others, $58 + \square = 100$ or $\square + 58 = 100$. Relate the language and reasoning to the mathematical symbols.*

Engage Observations:

- Did children associate the word *cent* with 100? Were they able to name other words beginning with cent—for example, centimeter, cent as used in money, century, etc.?
- Were they curious as to why a centipede has that name when it doesn't have 100 legs?
- Were children able to justify mathematically that the centipede had 42 legs?
- Were they able to follow the reasoning of those who wrote a different equation and used different reasoning than they did?

Explore:

Task A (Partners, Whole Group):

Resources: Counters, linking cubes or base ten blocks

- Present the following problem. Partners discuss the problem, develop a plan, and find a solution.
  - If the centipede has 34 shoes left over, how many legs does he have? Record the answer, using words, an equation, and a drawing.
- Share solutions and reasoning used to find the solution. Record equations, and relate them to the problem information and the solution.
- Repeat for the following problems:
  - When the centipede tries on his 42 shoes, he finds that 27 of them are too tight. How many are not too tight?
  - Two centipedes are crawling along a river bank. One gets mud on 35 of her feet. The other gets mud on 23 of her feet. How many feet have mud on them?

Task B (Partners, Whole Group):

Note: *Before doing this problem have children research the number of legs (feet) each animal below has and record number on class chart.*

Resources: Multiple copies of *Centipede's 100 Shoes*, counters, and base ten materials

- Read together, "He gave shoes to five spiders, four beetles, two woodlice, and a grasshopper with socks for the five spiders, and with enough shoes and socks left . . . for two worms."
- Refer to the chart listing the number of feet for these creatures.

- Ask the children to do the following:
  - ○ Using drawings, words, and numbers show how the centipede gave away all 100 of his shoes and all of his socks.
- Record the solution and share. Explain reasoning and compare with others.

Explore Observations:

- Do the children use concrete materials to find solutions to the problems?
- Can they find solutions but are unable to write the equations?
- Do they understand that there could be more than one way to write an equation for a problem?
- What strategies do they use to find the total feet of all the creatures? Do they make a chart?
- Are they listening and asking questions when other children are explaining their reasoning?
- Do they understand that ☐ represents the number they are looking for?

Consolidate:

Task A (Partners, Whole Group):

Resources: Centipede Word Problems (Appendix D [1])

- Over a period of time assign partners selected problems from **Centipede Word Problems.** Take time to share and justify solutions with the whole group asking such questions as the following:
  - ○ Can you tell us more about how you decided to do it that way?
  - ○ Did anyone do it differently? Tell us about it.
  - ○ Do you agree with what (child's name) said? Tell us why.
  - ○ Do you have a question you would like to ask them?
  - ○ I notice you got stuck when you were working on the problem. Do you want to tell us what you did to get unstuck?
  - ○ Does that make sense to you? Why?
  - ○ Have you seen a problem like this before? When?
  - ○ How did you decide what to do first?

Task B (Partners, Whole Group):

Resource: Centipede's Cousin Looney (Appendix D [2]).

- Give **Centipede's Cousin Looney** to each child. When finished, share solutions.

Task C (Individual, Partners):

- Write a word problem about the centipede.
- Write the solution on the back of the paper.

- Give the word problem to a partner to solve.
- Post problems for others to solve at center time.

Task D (Individual, Partners, Whole Group):

- Ask partners to complete **What Is the Question?** (Appendix D [3]).
- When all have an opportunity to complete **What Is the Question?** share with the whole group, justifying answers.

Consolidate Observations:

- What strategies are used to find solutions to the problems?
- Do children find putting together and taking away easier to do than other types, such as comparison, adding to, how many more needed, start number unknown, and change number unknown?
- Can they write the equation used to find a solution to the problem?
- Can they relate the equation to the actions with concrete materials or with their drawings?
- Do they show number sense in choosing numbers to fill the blanks in the story problem?
- When they write a word problem, do they include factual information that is usable to find a solution to the problem?
- Do they write a question that is answerable from the facts they included in their problem?
- What strategies do they use to write a question when they are given the answer?

Extend:

Task A (Individual, Whole Group):

- The centipede is looking out from under the log and sees some creatures go by. He counts 60 legs in total. Some legs are wood lice and some are beetles. How many of each is there?
- Share and compare solutions.

Task B (Partners, Whole Group):

- Surf the web for information about millipedes, and record on a chart. Create word problems based on the information.

Task C (Small Groups, Whole Group):

- Surf the web and books to find other insects that have more than 4 legs (feet).
- List the insects and number of legs (feet) each has.
- Choose at least 3 of these insects and provide at least 5 facts for each.
- Present a poster session; include a sketch or photo of the selected insects along with the facts, etc.
- Display.

Reflections and Discussion:

Children (Individual, Whole Group, Teacher-Posed Questions):

- Do you like or dislike anything in particular about *Centipede's 100 Shoes*? What is it and why?
- Would you recommend this book to a friend? Why or why not?
- What problems did you find most challenging?

Teacher(s) (If possible, share and discuss responses with colleagues.):

- What aspects of the **Investigation** do your children find most challenging? Why do you think that is so?
- Were the children more comfortable with addition or subtraction word problems?
- Did the children find some types of subtraction word problems easier than others?
- What strategies did they use to find solutions to the word problems?
- Did they listen to others share their solutions to problems?
- What changes would you make to this **Investigation**?
- What other areas of your curriculum could you use this book? How?

NUMBERS 10 TO 19/PLACE VALUE

Let's Count

Tana Hoban

Summary: Noted author–photographer Tana Hoban's counting book invites children to count from 1 to 15, spring to 20 and count by 10s to 50, then vault to 100. For each number a crisp, well-defined colored photo of simple—for example, 1 hen, 2 ice creams—to more sophisticated everyday things—for example, 20 mannequin heads each wearing a different hat and sunglasses—is presented on the right side of each double-page spread. On the left side of the spread is an enlarged yellow numeral, the word for the number printed in white uppercase letters and, as well, large white dots arranged to show the base ten representation of the number. *Let's Count* is eye-catching and engaging and is well worth revisiting many times.

INVESTIGATION A: NUMBERS 10 TO 19

Mathematics and Literature Experiences

Learning Expectations:

- To relate numerals 11 to 19 to 10s and 1, recognizing both the linguistic structure of the number names and place value representation
- To represent and describe numbers from 11 to 19 concretely, graphically, and symbolically
- To learn how visual language communicates ideas and shapes thought and action

Learning Resources: Multiple copies of *Let's Count*, linking cubes, and **10-Frames**

Read Aloud (Whole Group, Teacher as Reader):

- Explore and discuss the book jacket—its title, author–photographer's name and roles, what the book may be about, and why.
- Talk about the difference between an illustration and a photograph.
- Read the entire book, providing time to view each double-page spread.

Note: *As the book is being read, point to the specific text to provide guidance.*

- Place multiple copies of *Let's Count* in the math center for independent, peer, and home reading.

Engage:

Task A (Partners, Whole Group):

- Whole group rote count together from 1 to 20.
- Take turns repeating same with partner.

Task B (Individual, Partners):

- Revisit double-page spread for 10, and share what is depicted; continue to 15.
- Return to illustration for 12.
- Ask the following question:
  - o What number do you see? (Point to 12.)
  - o Point to the word *twelve*; say the word together.
- Point to the dots.
- Ask the following questions:
  - o How many dots? Allow time to count, if necessary.
  - o What do you notice about the way the dots are arranged?
  - o Why do you think the author arranged them this way?
  - o Ask a child to give you 12 linking cubes, and then arrange them as illustrated in the book (10 ones and 2 ones).
  - o Take the 10 ones, join them together, and call it a tower. Place the two other cubes next to it.
  - o Have children make the same.
- Ask the following questions:
  - o Point to the tower and ask, What else could we call it (1 ten; 10 ones)?
  - o Point to the numeral 12, and ask, How is the 10 ones tower and the 2 ones related to the symbols?
  - o If you placed the 1 ten tower over the numeral, where would you place it? Where would you place the 2 ones?
  - o Take time to discuss and say together 12 is the same as 1 ten and 2 ones, pointing to corresponding cubes.

- Record the following:

  12 = 1 ten and 2 ones

  12 = 1 ten + 2 ones

  12 = 10 + 2

- Repeat for 13, 14, 15, and then 11 and 10.
- Print the numerals 10 to 15 in random order; together say the number name.
- Ask the following question:
  - What do you notice about how the names for 14 and 15 are pronounced?

Note: *The number names for 14 to 19 can cause problems for children because, for example, when we say 14, we hear 4 first then the teen (ten); when we write the numeral we see the 10 first and then the 4. Often children write 41 instead of 14 for fourteen. They write what they hear.*

Note: *The number names for 11, 12, and 13 also need special attention—for example, 11 does not sound like the place value representation, namely, 1 ten and one and similarly for 12 and 13. Time needs to be spent relating the words to the symbols.*

Engage Observations:

- Can they name the numeral and read the number word as shown in *Let's Count*?
- Do they see the connection between the dot representation of the number, the symbol, and the number word?
- Do they connect the representation of the dots (one group of ten and ones) with the place value representation of the numeral?
- Does representing the numbers with linking cubes help children see place value representation of the numeral?
- Do children find the number names for 11 to 15 confusing? What strategies do they have to help them remember?

Explore:

Task A (Partners):

- Call the numbers 11 to 15 in random order; children print the numeral. Partners check each other's work.
- Write the number names 11 to15 in random order and children print the numeral. Partners check each other's work.
- Call the numbers 11 to 15 in random order, and children print the number name. Partners check each other's work.

Task B (Individual, Partners):

- Revisit the double-page spread for 15 in *Let's Count*.
- Ask the following question:
  - What number do you predict is on the next page?
- Turn to the next page, and discuss why Tana Hoban illustrated 20 rather than 16.
- Together recite the missing numbers between 15 and 20.
- Each child selects one of 16, 17, 18, 19 and illustrates it similar to the left-hand side illustrations in *Let's Count*.
- Represent each number with linking cubes and place by the corresponding illustration.
- Check each other's work.

Task C (Individual, Partners):

- Repeat **Task A** for the numbers 16 to 19.

Task D (Partners):

- Children take turns representing the numbers 10 to 19 on **10-Frames**.

Explore Observations:

- Are the children able to make the connections between the different representations of the numbers 10 to 19 (words, symbols, place value formats)?
- When the number name for each of 11 to 19 is called, can they write the correct symbol (e.g., do they write 16 for sixteen and not 61)?

Consolidate:

Task A (Partners):

Resource: Tub of linking cubes

- Ask the children to do the following:
  - Count out 14 cubes. Print the numeral for the number of cubes.
  - Make a group of 10 from the cubes; pull them aside. Show group of 10 and 4 ones.
  - Say: "We have fourteen cubes. Do you agree?"
  - Point to the 1 on the printed numeral.
  - Ask: "Where is this 1 shown in the cubes?"
  - Point to the 4; Ask: "Where is the 4 shown in the cubes?"
- Repeat for other numbers between 11 and 19.

Task B (Individual):

- Complete **Representing Numbers in Different Ways** (Appendix D [4]).

Numeral	Number Name	Drawing with Cubes
16		
19		
	fourteen	
		■■■■■■■■■ ■
12		
	seventeen	
		■■■■■■■■■■ ■■■
18		

Task C (Individual):

- Complete **Place Value Representations** (Appendix D [5]).

Numeral	_____ tens and _____ ones	10 + _____
16	1 ten and 6 ones	10 + 6
19		
	1 ten and 1 one	
		10 + 7
12		
	1 ten and 8 ones	
14		
		10 + 5
10		
	1 ten and 3 ones	

Consolidate Observations:

- Are children able to connect the digits in a two-digit numeral (10–19) with the corresponding number of cubes?
- Are children able to draw the correct number of objects for a given number? Do they use grouping to keep count?
- Are they able to represent numbers (10–19) in different ways, making place value connections?

Extend:

Task A (Individual, Whole Group):

- In the book revisit the right-hand illustration for 14.
- Ask the following question:
  - o What do you see?
- Count the objects, give responses, and record.
  Here are examples:
  - o There are 14 bins.
  - o Six bins are red, 4 are blue, and 4 are yellow.
  - o You can write the different groups as $3 + 3 + 4 + 4 = 14$.
  - o You can write the different groups as $6 + 4 + 4 = 14$.
- After each response, ask a child to explain how they counted.
- Revisit the right-hand illustration for 14; note the different representations and how they are connected.
- Assign a number (10 to 15) to each child to represent using an object of choice and grouping of the objects to make it easier to count.
- Encourage children to not only draw pictures but write addition equations, symbols, and place value notation and also include the numeral and the number name.
- Children may revisit *Let's Count* double-page spreads to note how the author–illustrator depicted the number.
- Group children with the same number and share the different ways they represented the number.
- Display the illustrations.

Task B (Individual, Small Groups, Whole Group):

- Research why 11 is named *eleven?*
- Share findings.

Note: *The word* eleven *comes from the old German word* ainlif, *meaning "one left." If you count using your fingers and thumbs, 11 is the first number of the next round, represented by a single digit left on its own. The word* twelve *is formed the same way: it means "two left." Lithuanian numbers are also formed in this way:* vienio-lika *"eleven,"* dvy-lika *"twelve,"* try-lika *"thirteen,"* keturio-lika *"fourteen."*

Reflection and Discussion:

Children (Individual, Whole Group, Teacher-Posed Questions):

- Share some strategies you have for remembering how to print the numeral for eleven, twelve, and thirteen?
- Does writing the number name for 14 confuse you? Why or why not?
- What did you learn from listening to your peers tell about their illustrated number?
- What is something you did in mathematics today that made you feel good?

Teacher (If possible, share and discuss responses with colleagues.):

- Have you spent focused time on tasks for the numbers 11 to 19? Why or why not? Do you think it is necessary?
- What did you like and dislike about this **Investigation**?
- What would you change the next time it is used?
- What are you left wondering about after doing this **Investigation**?
- What did you learn about children's understanding of place value?
- Did children enjoy revisiting independently or with a partner *Let's Count*?

NUMBERS 20 TO 100/PLACE VALUE

Let's Count

Tana Hoban

Summary: Noted author–photographer Tana Hoban's counting book invites children to count from 1 to 15, spring to 20 and count by 10s to 50, then vault to 100. For each number a crisp, well-defined colored photo of simple—for example, 1 hen, 2 ice creams—to more sophisticated everyday things—for example, 20 mannequin heads each wearing a different hat and sunglasses—is presented on the right side of each double-page spread. On the left side of the spread is an enlarged yellow numeral, the word for the number printed in white uppercase letters and, as well, large white dots arranged to show the base ten representation of the number. *Let's Count* is eye-catching and engaging and is well worth revisiting many times.

INVESTIGATION B: NUMBERS BETWEEN 20 and 100

Mathematics and Literature Experiences

Learning Expectations:

- To count to 100 by 10s and 1s
- To model two-digit numbers between 10 and 100 using multiple models to develop initial understanding of place value and the base ten system
- To find 10 more or 10 less than a two-digit number without counting and explain why
- To revisit and read together a familiar text for enjoyment and additional understanding

Learning Resources: Multiple copies of *Let's Count* and counters

Read Aloud (Teacher and Children as Readers):

- Reread together *Let's Count*.

Engage:

Note: *Children became familiar with* Let's Count *when engaged in* Let's Count ***Investigation A.***

Task A (Partners):

Resources: Copies of *Let's Count* and **100s Chart** (Appendix E [2]).

- Revisit the double-page spread for 20; read together the numbers on each spread to 100.
- Ask the following question:
  - What do you notice? Allow time to express ideas:

    Here are some examples:
  - We counted by 10s.
  - We missed some numbers.
  - The pattern was broken after 50.
  - When counting by 10s, numbers between 50 and 100 are missing.
  - These numbers are missing: 60, 70, 80, 90.
  - There are other numbers missing 21, 22, 23, etc.
- Why do you think the author skipped from 50 to 100? Allow time to express ideas, especially focusing on relationship between 50 and 100.
- Partners have a **100s Chart**.
- Ask the children to do the following:
  - Look at the column on the **100s Chart** that begins with 10.
  - Read together the numbers in the column: 10, 20, 30 . . . 100.
  - What do you notice about these numbers? Record.
  - Together, count from 1 to 100. When multiples of 10 are reached, do not say the number but clap your hands—for example, 9, clap; . . . 19, clap; . . . 99, clap.
  - Repeat.
- Why do you want to know how to count by 10s?

Task B (Individual, Partners):

Resources: Tub of base ten blocks (unit cubes, rod)

Note: *If children have not used the base ten blocks previously allow time to become familiar with them. In this **Investigation** the small cube is called a "one block" and the 10 ones joined together is called a "ten block." (If children call them by other names integrate these names into the **Task.**)*

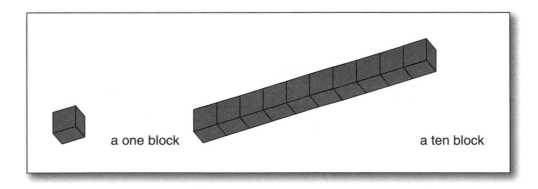

a one block   a ten block

- Return to *Let's Count* and the illustrations for 20 on left-hand page.
- Discuss the three representations of the number.
- Count the dots, the base ten representation of the number.
- Ask the following questions:
    - Why do you think the author arranged the dots in columns?
    - How many dots are in each column?
- Point to digit 2.
- Ask the following questions:
    - Where is the 2 represented in the dots?
    - Where is the 0?
- The conversation should center on the fact that the 2 is really 2 tens, and the two tens are represented by the two columns of ten dots. Run finger over the 2 and then the 2 columns of dots.
- Say, "There are no leftover dots. There are no ones. So we write zero (0) to show that."
- Ask the children to do the following:
    - Show the dots on the page with your one cubes. Arrange them as in *Let's Count*.
    - How many groups of ten can you make? Are there any left over?
    - Print the number that shows how many one blocks.
- Ask the following question:
    - If we were to trade the 20 one blocks for a ten block, how many ten blocks do you predict we will have?
- Allow time for children to check their prediction. Partners check each other's work.
- Discuss, sharing why the two different representations (20 one blocks and 2 ten blocks) are both 20.
- Say together, "Twenty one blocks is the same as 2 ten blocks. The name of the number is twenty." Print 20.
- Ask the following question:
    - What number do we have when we place a one block next to the 2 ten blocks?
    - Record the numeral (21); children do the same.
- Partners continue taking turns adding blocks and printing the corresponding numeral. When the tenth units cube is added, ask the following:
    - What number do you have now? Discuss, giving both answers and explanations (10 one blocks are traded for 1 ten block, and now you have 3 tens altogether).
- Print the numeral for 3 tens. If some write 210, talk about why that might have happened and bring attention to why it is written as 30.
- Children continue adding one blocks, and printing the number until they reach 40.

Engage Observations:

- How fluent are the children in counting to 100 by 1s, by 10s?
- Can children make the connection between the digits in 20 and the pictorial representation in the book?
- Do children understand that the 2 in the number 20 is 2 tens? The 0 is 0 ones.
- Can children associate the digits in a two-digit number with the concrete representation?
- Can they print the number for 4 tens? Do any write 410?

Explore:

Task A (Partners):

Resources: Copies of *Let's Count* and base ten blocks (one and ten blocks)

- Revisit the illustrations for 40.
- Ask the following questions:
  - o What number do you predict is on the next page? Check (50).
  - o Are there numbers omitted between 40 and 50?

Note: *Some may say "no" because there is not if you are counting by 10s. Others might say if you were counting by 1s then 41, 42, 43, 44, 45, 46, 47, 48, 49 are omitted. Discuss.*

- Choose one of these numbers—for example, 43.
- Ask partners to show 43 using only one blocks. Recheck, counting for accuracy.
- Ask the following questions:
  - o Can you form groups of ten with your blocks? Allow time to do so.
  - o Trade your groups for ten blocks.
  - o How many ten blocks? How many one blocks?
  - o If we trade these ten blocks into ones and count by ones, how many would we have? Together complete the following:

    Write the number that tells how many blocks? _____

    Write the number name: _____

    Complete: _____ tens _____ ones _____

- Partners repeat the previous **Task** for other numbers of their choice between 20 and 100.

Note: *When children trade the one blocks for tens and ones, ask questions to determine if children think they have the same number of blocks. Some children are challenged to understand that the count for 43 one blocks is the same as the count* *for 4 ten blocks and 3 ones. They have to make sense of it themselves by many opportunities to count and recount objects and talk about what they are doing. They usually will not learn it by being told.*

Variation: At a center provide containers of objects (between 20 and 100) and a recording sheet. Partners count the number of objects in a bag, rechecking each other's count. Record the number. Represent the number using base ten materials.

Task B (Partners):

Resource: Base ten blocks

- Ask the children to do the following:
  - o Make the number 57 using "one and ten blocks."
  - o Add 1 ten block.
  - o What number do you have now? Print it.
  - o What changed in the number? What stayed the same? Why?

  Here are some sample responses:

  - o You have one more ten because you added a ten block.
  - o The tens digit changed from 5 to 6 because you added one ten.
  - o The 7 stayed the same because you added a ten, not a one block.
- Repeat, asking children to take away a number of ten blocks from the 67.
- Repeat, asking to add and subtract one block.
- Repeat, using different start numbers.

Task C (Partners):

Resource: 100s Chart (Appendix E [2]) and transparent counters

- Partners share a copy of a **100s Chart**.
- Ask the children to do the following:
  - o Place a transparent marker on the number 25. Count 10 more. What number did you land on? Place a counter on it.
- Say together, "The number 25 and 10 more is 35." Record 25 + 10 = 35.
- Partners take turns picking numbers on the **100s Chart**, covering with transparent marker and adding 10 more. Record findings as an addition equation. Allow at least two turns each.
- Repeat for counting back 10. Record subtraction equations. Allow at least two turns each.
- Summarize findings by asking the following:
  - o How can you use the **100s Chart** to help you add and subtract 10 from a given number?

Task D (Individual, Whole Group):

- Call numbers between 10 and 100, and ask children in turn to say the number that is 10 more or 10 less than the number called.

Explore Observations:

- Do children understand that an arrangement of one blocks is the same count when rearranged as ten and one blocks?
- Do children connect the adding of a ten block or subtraction of a ten block with the symbolic representation? Can they do the same on the **100s Chart**?
- Can they write the corresponding addition and subtraction equations for the increase and decrease of a ten on the **100s Chart**?
- Can children orally and fluently add and subtract 10 from a given number?

Consolidate:

Task A (Partners):

Resources: Four-function calculator and **How Do I Get the Number?** (Appendix D [6])

- Key the start number into your calculator.
- Without pressing Clear, get the next number listed in the left-hand column on the chart.
- Write what you did (added or subtracted and by how much) to get it.

Start with 23	This is what I added or subtracted:
33	Example: I added 10.
23	
53	
73	
23	
13	
113	

Note: *This **Task** may be completed by using a **100s Chart** instead of a calculator.*

Task B (Individual):

- Design a double-page spread for the number 65.
- Represent 65 in many different ways, including different ways the number can be grouped.
- Share double-spread pages and display.

Task C (Individual, Partners, Whole Group):

Resource: Riddles (Appendix D [7])

- Complete **Riddles.** When everyone has had an opportunity to complete the sheet, share and discuss solutions with the whole group.

Task D (Partners, Whole Group):

Resources: Two number cubes: one labeled 1, 1, 1, 10, 10, 10 and the other is labeled +, +, +, −, −, −; score sheet **First to Reach 0 or 100** (Appendix D [8]).

- Model one game with the whole group.
- Each child has a score sheet; chooses a start number and writes it on the first line of the first column.
- In turn, each child rolls the two cubes, adds or subtracts (according to operation rolled) the number on the face of the cubes to the start number, and records the new number in the second column.
- New number is now the start number for the next round. Write it in the Start Number column
- Partners check each other's answers.
- The first child to reach 0 or 100 is the winner.
- Repeat.

First to Reach 0 or 100

Start Number	New Number		Start Number	New Number

Consolidate Observations:

- Are the children able to determine the number needed to move from one number to another, or do they have to make several tries on their calculator?
- How accurate are children in counting objects and showing them with base ten blocks?
- When they group the objects, do they think of tens and ones?
- Do they realize that the objects when counted by ones are the same count as when they grouped the blocks?
- Can they connect the expansion of a number in tens and ones with the numeral?
- In playing the game **First to Reach 0 or 100,** are they fluent in adding and subtracting tens?

Extend:

Task A (Individuals, Whole Group):

Resource: Base ten blocks

- Ask the children to do the following:
  - o Show 53 with the ones blocks. Check the count.
  - o How many different ways can you show 53 using the ten and one blocks?
  - Examples:
  - o 5 tens and 3 ones
  - o 4 tens and 13 ones
  - o 3 tens and 23 ones
  - o 2 tens and 33 ones
  - o 1 ten and 43 ones
- Share findings and justifications as to why each way makes sense.
- Repeat for other numbers.

Task B (Partners, Whole Groups):

- Plan an author–photographer study.
- Find books by Tana Hoban—for example, *Cubes, Cones, Cylinders, & Spheres; Shapes, Shapes, Shapes; More, Fewer, Less*—and create a book display.
- Partners select a book; plan and give a book talk.
- Make an author–photographer web of ideas—that is, list tasks and a book or books to be used to complete each.
- Partners complete specific task(s), and share with the whole group.
- Display final products.

Reflection and Discussion:

Children (Individual, Whole Group, Teacher-Posed Questions):

- Do you think the photographs were appropriate for *Let's Count?* Why or why not?
- What **Task** did you like best in this **Investigation**? Why?
- Why do you think it is important to know how to write numbers in different ways?
- Why do you think it is important to add or subtract by 10s?
- Did you do something today that you did not do before in mathematics?

Teacher(s) (If possible, share and discuss responses with colleagues.):

- It is often said that for children to truly understand that when sets of objects are grouped in different ways and the count is the same that they need to construct this relationship themselves through many counting activities and reflection on the results and not by being told by the teacher. Do you agree? Share experiences.
- What other ideas than those used in this **Investigation** for using the **100s Chart** help children learn place value concepts?

Appendices

APPENDIX A (1)

The Water Hole Investigation: Matching Numeral, Word, and Animal

Name: _____ **Date:** _____

Complete the following chart:

Numeral	Number Word	Animal Drawing
	one	
2		
	four	
5		

APPENDIX A (2)

5-Frame

APPENDIX A (3)

How Many Snails? A Counting Book Investigation: Language Pattern Chart

Language Pattern Chart

Questions	First Page	Second Page	Third Page	Child(ren's) Page
What are the first three words on each page?				
What are the first two words of each question?				
How many questions are on each page?				

APPENDIX A (4)

Ten Little Fish Investigation: Word Problems

Provide partners with a copy of each of the word problems.

Names: _____

A. The aquarium in the pet store is filled with 10 goldfish. Holly bought 1. How many goldfish are left in the aquarium?

Show how you found your answer using drawings, numbers, and symbols.

Names: _____

B. When Holly left the store, Jackson and Chris came to the store. Jackson bought 1 goldfish and Chris bought 1. How many are left in the aquarium now?

Show how you found your answer using drawings, numbers, and symbols.

Names: _____

C. There are 7 rabbits in the pen. The gate is left open and some rabbits run away. Now there are 5 rabbits in the pen. How many rabbits ran away?

Show how you found your answer using drawings, numbers, and symbols.

Names: _____

D. There are 12 pigeons in the park. A dog runs by and frightens them. First, one flies away, then another one, and then one more. How many pigeons are left? Show how you found your answer using drawings, numbers, and symbols.

APPENDIX B (1)

Ten Flashing Fireflies Investigation: Fireflies

Name: _____ **Date:** _____

Fireflies

In the Summer Night	In the Jar	Equations
10	0	
	1	
	2	
7		
	5	
4		
3		
	8	
1		
0		

APPENDIX B (2)

Ten Flashing Fireflies Investigation: Make 10

Name: _____ **Date:** _____

Complete the equations. Check answers with a partner.

A. 4 + _____ = 10

B. _____ + 8 = 10

C. 5 + _____ = 10

D. 2 + _____ = 10

E. 10 = _____ + 10

F. 1 + _____ = 10

G. _____ + 3 = 10

Write each equation as a subtraction equation with the unknown number on the right-hand side of the equation.

APPENDIX B (3)

Ten Flashing Fireflies Investigation: Matching

Name: _____ **Date:** _____

- Choose the letter (A, B, C . . .) corresponding to the equation in Column 2 that matches the equation in Column 1. Write the letter in the blank in Column 1.

Column 1	Column 2
$10 - \square = 6$ _____	A. $10 - 3 = \square$
$1 + 9 = \square$ _____	B. $\square + 8 = 10$
$2 + \square = 10$ _____	C. $10 - 5 = \square$
$5 + \square = 10$ _____	D. $6 + \square = 10$
$3 + \square = 10$ _____	E. $10 - \square = 1$
$10 - \square = 4$ _____	F. $10 - 2 = \square$
$10 - 8 = \square$ _____	G. $4 + \square - 10$

APPENDIX B (4)

365 Penguins Investigation: Lining Up Tiles

Names: _____ **and** _____ **Date:** _____

Day	Number of tiles	Every tile can be lined up in 2s with none left over.	One left over
1	1	no	yes
2	2	yes	no
3	3		

APPENDIX B (5)

365 Penguins Investigation: Adding Even Numbers

Names: _____ **and** _____ **Date:** _____

Complete the following chart:

+	2	4	6	8	10
2					
4					
6					
8					
10					

What do you notice?

APPENDIX B (6)

365 Penguins Investigation: Adding Odd Numbers

Names: _____ **and** _____ **Date:** _____

Complete the following chart:

+	1	3	5	7	9
1					
3					
5					
7					
9					

What do you notice?

APPENDIX B (7)

Four 100s Charts

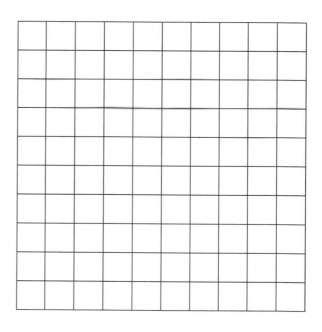

APPENDIX B (8)

Two Ways to Count to Ten: A Liberian Folktale Investigation: How Many?

How Many?

Name: _____ **and** _____

Name of container:

We counted by 1s, and there were _____.

We counted by _____, and there were _____.

We counted by _____, and there were _____.

This is what we learned:

This is what we are wondering about:

APPENDIX B (9)

Two Ways to Count to Ten: A Liberian Folktale Investigation: Numbers in Common

Numbers in Common

Names: _____, and _____ **Date:** _____

The leopard and the giraffe started to count at the same time.

The leopard counted by 2s and the giraffe by 5s.

They both agreed to stop when they reached 50.

What numbers did both the leopard and giraffe say?

You can use a **100s Chart** to help with your counting.

Record the numbers the leopard and giraffe counted.

Leopard:

Giraffe:

Circle the numbers that both the leopard and giraffe counted.
What do you notice about these numbers?

If the animals continued counting to 100 what numbers would both the leopard and giraffe say?

_____

_____

Write your own problem similar to the one just stated. Choose two different animals. Try to use different skip counting numbers.

APPENDIX B (10)

Minnie's Diner: A Multiplying Menu Investigation: How Many Pies?

Name: _____ **Date:** _____

Complete the chart to show how many each of the other brothers and the father will receive if the following occurs:

- Will orders 2 cherry pies when he first comes in the diner.
- Will orders 3 cherry pies when he first comes in the diner.
- Will orders 4 cherry pies when he first comes in the diner.
- Will orders 10 cherry pies when he first comes in the diner.

Will	Bill	Phil	Gill	Dill	Papa
1	2	4	8	16	32
2					
3					
4					
10					

APPENDIX B (11)

Minnie's Diner: A Multiplying Menu Investigation: Double or Add 2

Name: _____ **Date:** _____

	Number Put in Magic Purse A	**Magic Purse A**	**Money Put in Magic Purse B**	**Magic Purse B**
1st Try	1		1	
2nd Try				
3rd Try				
4th Try				
5th Try				
6th Try				

Which purse would you rather have?

APPENDIX B (12)

How Do You Count a Dozen Ducklings? Investigation: Equal Groups for 12

Name: _____ **Date:** _____

Directions: Partners choose 12 counters to represent the ducks. Take turns arranging the counters in as many equal groups as possible. Sketch groupings.

Write corresponding addition and multiplication equations for each grouping

12	**12**
Addition Equation:	Addition Equation:
Multiplication Equation:	Multiplication Equation:
12	**12**
Addition Equation:	Addition Equation:
Multiplication Equation:	Multiplication Equation:

APPENDIX C (1)

Balancing Act/Equal Shmequal Investigation: Balance the Equation

Name: _____ **Date:** _____

Balance the Equation:

A. $2 + 6 = \square$

B. $4 + \square = 9$

C. $4 + 6 = 5 + \square$

D. $8 - 1 = 6 + \square$

E. $8 - \square = 3$

F. $\square + 4 = 5 + 8$

G. $\square = 7$

APPENDIX C (4)

What's the Difference? An Endangered Animal Subtraction Story Investigation: Endangered Animal Problems

These problems may be assigned to children at different times during the year.

Endangered Animal Problems:

With your partner discuss and make a plan for solving each problem. Record solutions, and include drawings, words, numbers, and equation.

I look into the nest and see some eaglets.

Two more fly into the nest.

Now there are 5 eaglets in the nest.

How many eaglets are in the nest to begin with?

Record the solution, and include drawings, words, numbers, and equation.

A den is full when there are 10 wolves in it.

Jon counts 6 running into the den.

Then he sees 3 walk out. And in a little while 5 run back in.

How many wolves are in the den?

Record the solution, and include drawings, words, numbers, and equation.

The lepidopterist is caring for 12 butterflies.

She gives some to her friend's zoo. Now she has 8 butterflies.

How many does she give to her friend?

Record the solution, and include drawings, words, numbers, and equation.

Fourteen prairie dogs are frolicking.

Eight of them run into the colony, and the rest stay playing on the grass.

How many prairie dogs are playing on the grass?

Record the solution, and include drawings, words, numbers, and equation.

A pen is full when there are 10 bats in it.

There are 4 bats in the pen already.

How many more bats can get in the pen before it is full?

Record the solution, and include drawings, words, numbers, and equation.

The zookeeper has two cages for transporting animals.

Each cage can hold 10 animals.

There are 8 animals in one and 7 animals in the other.

The zookeeper needs to put 5 more animals in cage

Does he have enough room? How do you know?

Record the solution, and include drawings, words, numbers, and equation.

APPENDIX C (5)

The Twelve Days of Summer Investigation: Number of Gifts

Name: _____ **Date:** _____

Complete the following chart:

Day	Number of Gifts	Total
First		
Second		
Third		
Fourth		
Fifth		
Sixth		
Seventh		
Eighth		
Ninth		
Tenth		
Eleventh		
Twelfth		

APPENDIX D (1)

Centipede's 100 Shoes Investigation: Centipede Word Problems

A. Centipede decides to give away the 58 leftover shoes. First, he shares them with 1 grasshopper and 2 beetles, one shoe for each of their feet.

How many shoes does the centipede have left to give to other creatures?

To which creatures could he give them?

- Record the solution; include drawings, words, numbers, and an equation.

B. When centipede's aunt knits 25 socks she wonders how many more she needs to knit to have enough for all of the centipede's 42 feet. How many more does she have to knit?

- Record the solution; include drawings, words, numbers, and an equation.

C. Crawley the centipede hides some shoes under the log. She gives 32 to her friend. Now she has 27 shoes. How many shoes did Crawley hide?

- Record the solution; include drawings, words, numbers, and an equation.

D. There are 27 centipedes under the log. Some crawl out from under leaves and join them. Now there are 53 centipedes. How many centipedes crawl out from under the leaves?

- Record the solution; include drawings, words, numbers, and an equation.

E. A centipede's mother buys him 27 shoes. His grandfather buys him 69. How many shoes does he have altogether? How many more shoes did his grandfather buy than his mother?

- Record the solution; include drawings, words, numbers, and an equation.

F. An old rotten log has space for 25 centipedes under it. There are already 13 hiding there. How many more can crawl in before the space under the log is filled?

- Record the solution; include drawings, words, numbers, and an equation.

APPENDIX D (2)

Centipede's 100 Shoes Investigation: Centipede's Cousin Looney

Name: _____ **Date:** _____

- Choose from the numbers in the box so that the story problem about the centipede's cousin named Looney makes sense.

> Numbers: 27, 78, 39, 11, 39, 51

At _____o'clock Looney, the centipede, goes to the store to buy _____shoes.

He wants _____for the left feet and _____for the right feet.

When he gets home _____shoes have laces and the rest have Velcro.

How many have Velcro? _____

- Share and discuss choices of numbers with the whole group.

APPENDIX D (3)

Centipede's 100 Shoes Investigation: What Is the Question?

What Is the Question?

Names: _____ **and** _____ **Date:** _____

You know the following:

- o Looney has 38 legs, and Creepy has 54 legs.
- o Crawley has 78 legs, and Eerie has 94 legs.

What is the question if the answer is as follows:

56

92

24

APPENDIX D (4)

Let's Count (A) Investigation: Representing Numbers in Different Ways

Name: _____ **Date:** _____

Complete the chart, and check answers with a partner.

Numeral	Number Name	Drawing with Cubes
16		
19		
	fourteen	
		■■■■■■■■■ ■
12		
	seventeen	
		■■■■■■■■■ ■■■
18		

APPENDIX D (5)

Let's Count (A) Investigation: Place Value Representations

Name: _____ **Date:** _____

Complete the chart and check answers with a partner.

Numeral	_____ tens and _____ ones	10 + _____
16	1 ten and 6 ones	10 + 6
19		
	1 ten and 1 one	
		10 + 7
12		
	1 ten and 8 ones	
14		
		10 + 5
10		
	1 ten and 3 ones	

APPENDIX D (6)

Let's Count (B) Investigation: How Do I Get the Number?

Name: _____ **Date:** _____

Key the start number into your calculator. Without pressing Clear, get the next number listed in the column on the chart. Tell what you did (added or subtracted and how much) to get it.

Start with 23	This is what I added or subtracted:
33	Example: I added 10.
23	
53	
73	
23	
13	
113	

APPENDIX D (7)

Let's Count (B) Investigation: Riddles

Name: _____ **Date:** _____

Complete the following riddles:

1. I have 73 ones. Who am I? _____

2. I have 30 ones and 6 tens. Who am I? _____

3. I have 3 tens and 17 ones. Who am I? _____

4. I have _____ ones. I have 3 tens. My number is 43.

5. I have 24 ones and 1 ten. What number do I have? _____

6. I have 5 tens and 15 ones. What number do I have? _____

7. My number is 99. How many more ones do I need to have 100? _____

8. I have _____ tens and 21 ones. My number is 51.

9. I have 4 tens and 26 ones. What number do I have? _____

10. Write 3 riddles of your own. Have a partner complete them.

APPENDIX D (8)

Let's Count (B) Investigation: First to Reach 0 or 100

Names: _____ **and** _____ **Date:** _____

Start Number	New Number		Start Number	New Number

APPENDIX E (1)

10-Frame

APPENDIX E (2)

100s Chart

1	2	3	4	5	6	7	8	9	10
11	12	13	14	15	16	17	18	19	20
21	22	23	24	25	26	27	28	29	30
31	32	33	34	35	36	37	38	39	40
41	42	43	44	45	46	47	48	49	50
51	52	53	54	55	56	57	58	59	60
61	62	63	64	65	66	67	68	69	70
71	72	73	74	75	76	77	78	79	80
81	82	83	84	85	86	87	88	89	90
91	92	93	94	95	96	97	98	99	100

APPENDIX F

Learning Expectations Correlation Chart

This chart presents the correlation between the Investigations' learning expectations and Common Core State Standards (CCSS) in mathematics and English language arts.

KEY:

- Mathematics Standards:

Abbreviations for standards are used in the following table, as stated in the CCSS document, e.g., MP1 is the abbreviated form of "make sense of problems and persevere in solving them"; K.CC.3 is the abbreviated form of Kindergarten: Counting and Cardinality Domain, Standard 3.

- English Language Arts Standards:
  o L (Language); RL (Reading: Literature); RI (Reading: Informational Text); RF (Reading: Foundational Skills); SL (Speaking & Listening); W (Writing)
  o K, 1, and 2 Grade Level
  o Specific standard number—that is, 1 is the first standard listed in each English language arts area
  o Here is an example: RL.K.1 means Reading: Literature Kindergarten First Standard

Learning Expectations	Common Core State Standards for Mathematics (CCSSM) Standards for Practice	CCSSM Standards for Content	Common Core State Standards for English Language Arts (CCSS.ELA)
UNIT I			
The Water Hole Investigation			
To solve quantitative problems, such as finding the number of objects in a pictorial representation or set and producing sets of a given size	MP1	K.CC. 5	
To represent numbers in multiple ways	MP4	K.CC .4	
To explore and connect mathematical language in a meaningful way	MP6		
To acquire information and build understanding from a nonfiction text			RL. K,1,2.1; RI. K,1,2.1&2
To create a written text using a familiar literary format			W. K,1,2.2&6
Olly and Me 1•2•3 Investigation			
To recognize quantities up to 10 by subitizing		K.CC.5	
To communicate strategies and skills used to recognize a quantity	MP3 MP6		
To develop spatial visualization skills	MP2		
To relate illustrations to the story as it unfolds			RL. K,1,2.7; RI. K,1,2.7
Mouse Count Investigation			
To count objects using one-to-one correspondence		K.CC.4a	
To count forward beginning from a given number within the known sequence (instead of having to begin at 1) and know last number named tells how many		K.CC.2	
To find out how many by "counting on" from a given number		K.CC.2	
To solve word problems involving the strategy of counting on to find the solution	MP1		

(Continued)

(Continued)

Learning Expectations	Common Core State Standards for Mathematics (CCSSM) Standards for Practice	CCSSM Standards for Content	Common Core State Standards for English Language Arts (CCSS.ELA)
To write equations for counting on and addition relationships	MP4	K.OA.1	
To share and discuss thoughts related to the story			SL. K,1,2.1
To ask and respond to questions			RL. K,1,2.1
To recognize common types of texts (concept book)			RL. K,1.5
How Many Snails? A Counting Book (A) Investigation			
To determine how many are in a set and part of a set		K.CC.4	
To represent numbers in different ways and make connections among the different representations	MP2		
To use spoken and written language to communicate mathematical reasoning coherently and effectively to others	MP6		SL.K,1,2.1; W.K,1,2.2
To recognize language patterns			
To develop concepts about print and an awareness of book language			RI.K.5 RF.K.1
Ten Little Fish Investigation			
To say the number sequence backwards by 1s, starting anywhere from 10 to 1, with and without concrete materials			
To solve word problems that relate counting backwards to subtraction	MP1	K.OA.2	
To model with mathematics	MP4		
To apply a range of strategies to comprehend texts			
To read poetic text to build an understanding of the genre and for personal fulfillment			RL. K,1,2.10

Learning Expectations	Common Core State Standards for Mathematics (CCSSM) Standards for Practice	CCSSM Standards for Content	Common Core State Standards for English Language Arts (CCSS.ELA)
UNIT II			
One Big Building: A Counting Book About Construction Investigation			
To compare two sets using one-to one correspondence and describe them, using comparative words such as *more than, fewer than,* or *same as*		K.CC.6; K.CC.7	
To compare a set to a given referent using comparative language			
To solve a given problem (pictures and words) that involves the comparison of two quantities	MP1		
To calculate how many more and how many fewer in given sets of objects			
To represent mathematical ideas in multiple ways	MP2		
To develop reading strategies, such as predicting, hypothesizing, and synthesizing			
To understand the meaning and use of punctuation marks			LA. K,1,2.2
How Many Snails? A Counting Book (B) Investigation			
To compare sets of objects for more than, less than, and equal to the number of objects in another group		K.CC.6	
To use appropriate language and symbolism to compare quantities and numbers less than 20	MP2	1.NBT.3	
To connect different representations of mathematical ideas	MP1		
To use spoken and written language to communicate coherently and effectively mathematical reasoning to various audiences	MP4		SL. K,1,2.1; W.K,1,2.2

(Continued)

(Continued)

Learning Expectations	Common Core State Standards for Mathematics (CCSSM) Standards for Practice	CCSSM Standards for Content	Common Core State Standards for English Language Arts (CCSS.ELA)
Ten Flashing Fireflies Investigation			
To find the number that makes 10, for any number from 1 to 9, when added to the given number, by using objects or drawings, and record the answer with a drawing or equation		K.OA.4	
To see the relationship between missing addends and subtraction		1.OA.4	
To model with mathematics and look for patterns to solve problems	MP4; MP1		
To recognize common types of texts—for example, poems			RL. K,1,2.5
To use illustrations to describe the setting			RL. K,1,2.7
To read poetry of appropriate complexity with prompting and support for grade level			RL. K,1,2.10
To become familiar with poetic language and structure			RL.2.4
365 Penguins Investigation			
To determine whether a group of objects has an odd or even number of members		2.OA.3	
To determine whether the sum of two even numbers, sum of two odd numbers, and sum of an even and an odd number is even or odd and to explain why		2.OA.3	
To make a generalization	MP3		
To identify who is telling/narrating the story			RL.1.6
To listen to stories to instill a sense of story			
To increase cognitive skills, including the ability to think critically			

Learning Expectations	Common Core State Standards for Mathematics (CCSSM) Standards for Practice	CCSSM Standards for Content	Common Core State Standards for English Language Arts (CCSS.ELA)
Two Ways to Count to Ten: A Liberian Folktale Investigation			
To skip count orally by 2s, 5s, and 10s to 100			
To use skip counting to count a number of objects			
To communicate reasoning to others	MP3		
To determine the central message, lesson, or moral of a folktale			RL.2.2
To read literary texts in a variety of genres			RL. K,1,2.10
Minnie's Diner: A Multiplying Menu Investigation			
To relate doubling to addition and multiplication by 2			
To compare doubling to adding 2 to a number			
To use patterns to solve problems	MP1		
To communicate reasoning to others	MP6		SL.K.6
To develop a sense of story			
To identify characters, settings, and key events in a story			RL.K,1.3
To relate illustrations to the overall story in which they appear			RL.K,1,2.7; RI.K,1,2.7
How Do You Count a Dozen Ducklings? Investigation			
To divide a number of objects into equal groups—concretely and pictorially—and record the corresponding addition and multiplication equations			
To connect equal groups and repeated addition to multiplication		2.OA.4	
To construct viable arguments and critique the reasoning of others	MP3		

(Continued)

(Continued)

Learning Expectations	Common Core State Standards for Mathematics (CCSSM) Standards for Practice	CCSSM Standards for Content	Common Core State Standards for English Language Arts (CCSS.ELA)
To use information gained from the illustrations and text to demonstrate understanding of the plot			RL.2.7
To increase ability to think critically			
To learn how visual language communicates ideas and shapes thought and action			RL.K,1,2.7
UNIT III			
Balancing Act/Equal Shmequal Investigation			
To develop an understanding of the equal sign and to understand equality in relation to a balanced scale		1.OA.7	
To solve equations written in different formats	MP2	1.OA.8	
To communicate reasoning to others	MP3		
To ask and answer questions with prompting and support about key details in a text			RL.K,1,2.3
To name the author and illustrator of a story and define the role of each			RL.K. 6
To experience different kinds of texts on the same topic			RI.K,1,29
Quack and Count Investigation			
To decompose numbers and write them as the sum of two other numbers in more than one way		K.NBT.1; 1.OA.1	
To demonstrate an understanding of equation as balance and the meaning of an equal sign		1.OA.7	
To solve word problems with three addends to 20	MP1	1.OA.2	
To make generalizations and use them to make predictions	MP3		

Learning Expectations	Common Core State Standards for Mathematics (CCSSM) Standards for Practice	CCSSM Standards for Content	Common Core State Standards for English Language Arts (CCSS.ELA)
To model with mathematics	MP4		
To represent mathematical ideas in multiple ways	MP4		
To explore and connect mathematical language in a meaningful context	MP6		
To use spoken and written language to communicate mathematical reasoning coherently and effectively to others	MP3		SL.K,1,2.1; W.K,1,2.2
To acquire information and build understanding from poetic text			
The Tub People Investigation			
To represent numbers up to 20 as the sum of two addends		K.OA.3	
To write equations to show the relationship between three or more numbers		1.OA.8	
To use 0 to tell how many in a set with no elements			
To find multiple solutions to a problem and represent solutions in multiple ways	MP1; MP2		
To look for patterns and make a generalization	MP3		
To increase cognitive abilities, including the ability to think critically			
To use spoken and written language to communicate mathematical reasoning coherently and effectively to others	MP3		SL.K,1,2.1; W.K,1,2.2
To provide a model of expressive, fluent reading			

(Continued)

(Continued)

Learning Expectations	Common Core State Standards for Mathematics (CCSSM) Standards for Practice	CCSSM Standards for Content	Common Core State Standards for English Language Arts (CCSS.ELA)
What's the Difference? An Endangered Animal Subtraction Story Investigation			
To use subtraction within 20 to solve word problems involving taking from, taking apart, and comparing, with unknowns in all positions, by using objects, drawings, and equations with a symbol for the unknown number to represent the problem		1.OA.1	
To understand subtraction as an unknown addend problem		1.OA.4	
To understand addition and subtraction as inverse operations		1.OA.4	
To make sense of problems and persevere in solving them	MP1		
To ask and answer questions about key details in a text			RL.K,1,2.1
To read prose and poetry of appropriate complexity with prompting and support			RL.K,1,2.10
To apply various comprehension and interpretative strategies to informational text			
The Twelve Days of Summer Investigation			
To demonstrate an understanding of addition of numbers concretely, pictorially, and symbolically		1.OA.1	
To describe and use personal strategies to find the sum of two or more addends		1.OA.3	
To solve word problems involving addition	MP1		
To communicate mathematical ideas and reasoning to others using appropriate everyday and mathematical language	MP3		SL.K,1,2.1; W.K,1,2.2
To relate the illustrations to the text			RL.K,1,2.7; RI.K,1,2.7

Learning Expectations	Common Core State Standards for Mathematics (CCSSM) Standards for Practice	CCSSM Standards for Content	Common Core State Standards for English Language Arts (CCSS.ELA)
UNIT IV			
One Is a Snail, Ten Is a Crab Investigation			
To represent and describe numbers to 100 concretely, pictorially, and symbolically using base ten and place value		1.NBT.1; 1.NBT.2; 2.OA.1	
To decompose numbers		K.OA.3; K.NBT.1	
To add two or more one- and two-digit numbers to get a given number		1.OA.1; 1.NBT.2; 1.OA.3	
To use spoken and written language to communicate mathematical reasoning coherently and effectively to others	MP.3		SL.K,1,2.1; W.K,1,2. 2
To read a wide range of literary genres to acquire information and build understanding, and for personal fulfillment			RL.K,1,2.10
Centipede's 100 Shoes Investigation			
To use addition and subtraction within 100 to solve one- and two-step word problems involving situations of adding to, taking from, putting together, taking apart, and comparing, with unknowns in all positions—for example, by using drawings and equations with a symbol for the unknown number to represent the problem		1.OA.1; 2.OA.1	
To communicate reasoning to others	MP3		
To actively engage in group reading with purpose and understanding			RL.K,1,2.10
To ask and answer questions about key details in a text			RL.K,1,2.1
To apply strategies to comprehend and interpret text			

(Continued)

(Continued)

Learning Expectations	Common Core State Standards for Mathematics (CCSSM) Standards for Practice	CCSSM Standards for Content	Common Core State Standards for English Language Arts (CCSS.ELA)
Let's Count (A) Investigation			
To relate numerals, 10 to 19, to 10s and 1, recognizing both the linguistic structure of the number names and place value representation		1.OA.2	
To represent and describe numbers from 11 to 19 concretely, graphically, and symbolically	MP4	1.OA.2	
To learn how visual language communicates ideas and shapes thought and action			RI.K,1,2. 7
Let's Count (B) Investigation			
To count to 100 by 10s and 1s		1.NBT.1	
To model two-digit numbers between 10 and 100 using multiple models to develop initial understanding of place value and the base ten system		1.NBT.2; 2.NBT.1,3	
To find 10 more or 10 less than a two-digit number without counting and explain why	MP3		
To revisit and read together a familiar text for enjoyment and additional understanding			RL.K,1,2.10

References

Andrews, J. (2007). *The twelve days of summer* (S. Jolliffe, Illus.). Victoria, BC: Orca.

Baker, K. (2004). *Quack and count.* Toronto, ON: Harcourt.

Baroody, A. J. (2000). Does mathematics instruction for 3 to 5 year olds really make sense? *Young Children, 55*(4), 61–67.

Base, G. (2004). *The water hole.* New York: Puffin.

Battista, M. T. (2002). Learning in an inquiry-based classroom: Fifth graders' enumeration of cubes in 3D arrays. In J. Sowder & B. Schappelle (Eds.), *Lessons learned from research.* Reston, VA: National Council of Teachers of Mathematics.

Booth, D. (1998). *Guiding the reading process.* Markham, ON: Pembroke.

Bruner, J. (1960). *The process of education.* London, UK: Oxford University.

Chae, I. S. (2006). *How do you count a dozen ducklings?* (S. H. Rew, Illus.). Park Ridge, IL: Albert Whitman.

Clements, D. H. (1999). Concrete manipulatives, concrete ideas. *Contemporary issues in early childhood, 1*(1), 45–60. Retrieved June 2010 from http://www.gse.buffalo.edu/org/buildingblocks/Newsletters/ConcreteYelland

Common Core State Standards Initiative. (2012a). *Common Core State Standards for English Language Arts.* Washington, DC: The National Governors Association Center for Best Practices and the Council of Chief State School Officers. Retrieved from http://www.corestandards.org/ELA-Literacy

Common Core State Standards Initiative. (2012b). *Common Core State Standards for Mathematics.* Washington, DC: The National Governors Association Center for Best Practices and the Council of Chief State School Officers. Retrieved from http://www.corestandards.org/

Conrad, P. (1995). *The tub people* (R. Egielski, Illus.). New York: Balzer & Bray.

Copley, J. V. (2000). *The young child and mathematics.* Washington, DC: National Association for the Education of Young Children.

Dacey, L., & Collins, A. (2010). *Zeroing in on number and operations.* Portland, ME: Stenhouse.

Dahl, M. (2005). *One big building: A counting book about construction* (T. Ouren, Illus.). Minneapolis, MN: Picture Window.

de la Mare, W. (1942). *Bells and grass.* New York: Viking.

Dee, R. (1988). *Two ways to count to ten: A Liberian folktale* (S. Meddaugh, Illus.). New York: Henry Holt.

Dodds, D. (2007). *Minnie's diner: A multiplying menu.* Cambridge, MA: Candlewick.

Donaldson, M. (1978). *Children's minds.* London: Fontana/Croom Helm.

Dosemagen, D. M. (2007). Shared reflection in an online environment: Exposing and promoting students' understanding. In W. G. Martin, M. E. Strutchens, & P. C. Elliott (Eds.), *The learning of mathematics, 69th yearbook.* Reston, VA: National Council of Teachers of Mathematics.

Freeman, E. B., & Goetz Person, D. (1998). *Connecting informational children's books with content area learning.* Toronto, ON: Allyn & Bacon.

Fromental, J.-L. (2006). *365 penguins* (J. Jolivet, Illus.). New York: Harry N. Abrams.

Giganti, P., Jr. (1994). *How many snails? A counting book* (D. Crews, Illus.). New York: Greenwillow.

Ginsburg, H. P., & Baron, J. (1993). Cognition: Young children's construction of mathematics. In R. J. Jensen (Ed.), *Research ideas for the classroom: Early childhood mathematics* (pp. 3–21). New York: Macmillan.

Griffiths, R., & Clyne, M. (1988). *Books you can count on: Linking mathematics and literature.* Portsmouth, NH: Heinemann.

Hancock, M. (2008). *A celebration of literature and response* (3rd ed.). Columbus, OH: Pearson.

Hiebert, J. (2003). Signposts for teaching mathematics through problem solving. In F. K. Lester Jr. (Ed.), *Teaching mathematics through problem solving: Prekindergarten– grade 6.* Reston, VA: National Council of Teachers of Mathematics.

Hiebert, J., Carpenter, T., Fennema, E., Fuson, K. C., Wearne, D., Murray, H., . . . Human, P. (1997). *Making sense: Teaching and learning mathematics with understanding.* Portsmouth, NH: Heinemann.

Hoban, T. (1999). *Let's count.* New York: Greenwillow.

Hughes, S. (2009). *Olly and me 1•2•3.* Somerville, MA: Candlewick.

Hunsader, P. (2004). Mathematics trade books: Establishing their value and assessing their quality. *The Reading Teacher, 57,* 618–629.

Kiefer, B., Hepler S., & Hickman, J. (2007). *Charlotte Huck's children's literature* (9th ed.). New York: McGraw-Hill.

Kilpatrick, J., Swafford, J., & Findell, B. (Eds.) (2001). *Adding it up: Helping children learn mathematics.* Washington, DC: National Academy Press.

Kroll, V. (2005). *Equal shmequal* (P. O'Neill, Illus.). Watertown, MA: Charlesbridge.

Langer, J. A. (1995). *Envisioning literature: Literary understanding and literature instruction.* New York: Teachers College.

Lynch-Brown, C., & Tomlinson, C. (2008). *Essentials of children's literature* (6th ed.). Boston: Pearson.

Morrow, L., & Gambrell, L. (2004). *Using children's literature in preschool: Comprehending and enjoying books.* Newark, DE: International Reading Association.

Moyer, P. S., Bolyard, J. J., & Spikell, M. A. (2002). *What are virtual manipulatives?* Retrieved from http://www.grsc.k12.ar.us/mathresources/instruction/manipulatives/ Virtual%20Manipulatives.pdf

National Council of Teachers of English & International Reading Association. (1996). *Standards for the English language arts.* Urbana, IL: Author.

National Council of Teachers of Mathematics. (1989). *The curriculum and assessment standards for school mathematics.* Reston, VA: Author.

National Council of Teachers of Mathematics. (2000). *Principles and standards for school mathematics.* Reston, VA: Author.

National Council of Teachers of Mathematics. (2001). *Professional standards for teaching mathematics.* Reston, VA: Author.

National Council of Teachers of Mathematics. (2006). *Curriculum focal points for prekindergarten through grade 8 mathematics.* Reston, VA: Author.

National Council of Teachers of Mathematics. (2007). *Mathematics teaching today.* Reston, VA: Author.

National Council of Teachers of Mathematics. (2010). *Developing essential understanding of number and numeration pre-K-2.* Reston, VA: Author.

Pappas, C., Kiefer, B., & Levstik, L. (1999). *An integrated language perspective in the elementary school: An action approach.* New York: Longman.

Perry, B., & Dockett, S. (2002). Young children's access to powerful mathematics ideas. In L. English (Ed.), *Handbook of international research in mathematics education* (2nd ed.) Mahwah, NJ: Lawrence Erlbaum.

Ross, T. (2003). *Centipede's 100 shoes.* New York: Henry Holt.

Sayre, A. P., & Sayre, J. (2010). *One is a snail, ten is a crab: A counting by feet book* (R. Cecil, Illus.). Cambridge, MA: Candlewick.

Schiro, M. (1997). *Integrating children's literature and mathematics in the classroom.* New York: Teachers College.

Slade, S. (2010). *What's the difference? An endangered animal subtraction story.* Mt. Pleasant, SC: Sylvan Dell.

Small, M., Sheffield, L. J., Cavanagh, M., Dacey, L., Findell, C. R., & Greenes, C. E. (2004). *Navigating through problem solving and reasoning in grade 2.* Reston, VA: National Council of Teachers of Mathematics.

Smith, M. S., & Stein, M. K. (2011). *Practices for orchestrating productive mathematics discussions.* Reston, VA: National Council of Teachers of Mathematics; Thousand Oaks, CA: Corwin.

Stice, C., Bertrand, J., & Bertrand, N. (1995). *Integrating reading and the other language arts.* Scarborough, ON: Thomas Nelson.

Strong, E. (1988). *Nurturing early literacy: A literature based program for at-risk first graders* (Unpublished doctoral dissertation). The Ohio State University, Columbus.

Sturges, P. (1997). *Ten flashing fireflies* (A. Vojtech, Illus.). New York: NorthSouth.

Van de Walle, J. A. (1998). *Elementary and middle school mathematics: Teaching developmentally* (3rd *ed.*). New York: Longman.

Van de Walle, J. A. (2003). Designing and teaching mathematics through problem solving. In F. K. Lester Jr. (Ed.), *Teaching mathematics through problem solving: Prekindergarten–grade 6.* Reston, VA: National Council of Teachers of Mathematics.

Vandergrift, K. E. (1986). *Child and story: The literary connection.* New York: Neal-Schuman.

Vygotsky, L. S. (1986). *Thought and language.* Cambridge, MA: MIT.

Walsh, E. (2001). *Mouse count.* New York: Houghton Mifflin Harcourt.

Walsh, E. (2010). *Balancing act.* New York: Beach Lane.

Whitin, D. J., & Whitin, P. (1996). Fostering metaphorical thinking through children's literature. In P. C. Elliott & M. J. Kenney (Eds.), *Communication in mathematics K–12 and beyond.* Reston, VA: National Council of Teachers of Mathematics.

Whitin, D. J., & Wilde, S. (1992). *Read any good math lately? Children's books for mathematics earning, K–6.* Portsmouth, NH: Heinemann.

Whitin, P., & Whitin, D. J. (2000). *Math is language too.* Urbana, IL: National Council of Teachers of English.

Whitin, D. J., & Whitin, P. (2004). *New visions for linking literature and mathematics.* Urbana, IL: National Council of Teachers of English.

Wood, A. (2004). *Ten little fish* (B. Wood, Illus.). New York: Scholastic.

Yackel, E. (2003). Listening to children: Informing us and guiding our instruction. In F. K. Lester Jr. (Ed.), *Teaching mathematics through problem solving: Prekindergarten–grade 6.* Reston, VA: National Council of Teachers of Mathematics.

Yackel, E., Cobb, P., Wood, T., Wheatley, G., & Merkel, G. (1990). The importance of social interaction in children's construction of mathematical knowledge. In T. Cooney (Ed.), *Teaching and learning mathematics in the 1990s: 1990 yearbook of the National Council of Teachers of Mathematics.* Reston, VA: National Council of Teachers of Mathematics.

Bibliography of Children's Literature for the Investigations

Andrews, J. (2007). *The twelve days of summer* (S. Jolliffe, Illus.). Victoria, BC: Orca.

Baker, K. (2004). *Quack and count.* Toronto, ON: Harcourt.

Base, G. (2004). *The water hole.* New York: Puffin.

Carle, E. (1987). *A house for hermit crab.* Natick, MA: Picture Book.

Chae, I. S. (2006). *How do you count a dozen ducklings?* (S. H. Rew, Illus.). Park Ridge, IL: Albert Whitman.

Conrad, P. (1995). *The tub people* (R. Egielski, Illus.). New York: Balzer & Bray.

Dahl, M. (2005). *One big building: A counting book about construction* (T. Ouren, Illus.). Minneapolis, MN: Picture Window.

Dee, R. (1988). *Two ways to count to ten: A Liberian folktale* (S. Meddaugh, Illus.). New York: Henry Holt.

Dodds, D. (2007). *Minnie's diner: A multiplying menu.* Cambridge, MA: Candlewick.

Fromental, J.-L. (2006). *365 penguins* (J. Jolivet, Illus.). New York: Harry N. Abrams.

Gibbons, G. (1992). *Stargazers.* New York: Holiday House.

Giganti, P., Jr. (1994). *How many snails? A counting book* (D. Crews, Illus.). New York: Greenwillow.

Hoban, T. (1999). *Let's count.* New York: Greenwillow.

Hughes, S. (2009). *Olly and me 1•2•3.* Somerville, MA: Candlewick.

Kroll, V. (2005). *Equal shmequal* (P. O'Neill, Illus.). Watertown, MA: Charlesbridge.

Merriam, E. (1993). *12 Ways to Get to 11* (B. Karlin, Illus.). New York: Simon & Schuster.

Ross, T. (2003). *Centipede's 100 shoes.* New York: Henry Holt.

Sayre, A. P., & Sayre, J. (2010). *One is a snail, ten is a crab: A counting by feet book* (R. Cecil, Illus.). Cambridge, MA: Candlewick.

Simon, S. (2006). *Stars.* New York: Programs and Genres.

Slade, S. (2010). *What's the difference? An endangered animal subtraction story.* Mt. Pleasant, SC: Sylvan Dell.

Sturges, P. (1997). *Ten flashing fireflies* (A. Vojtech, Illus.). New York: NorthSouth.

Tafuri, N. (2009). *The big storm: A very soggy counting book.* Toronto, ON: Simon & Schuster.

Walsh, E. (2001). *Mouse count.* New York: Houghton Mifflin Harcourt.

Walsh, E. (2010). *Balancing act.* New York: Beach Lane.

Wood, A. (2004). *Ten little fish* (B. Wood, Illus.). New York: Scholastic.

Index

CORWIN

A SAGE Company

The Corwin logo—a raven striding across an open book—represents the union of courage and learning. Corwin is committed to improving education for all learners by publishing books and other professional development resources for those serving the field of PreK–12 education. By providing practical, hands-on materials, Corwin continues to carry out the promise of its motto: **"Helping Educators Do Their Work Better."**

The National Council of Teachers of Mathematics is the public voice of mathematics education, supporting teachers to ensure equitable mathematics learning of the highest quality for all students through vision, leadership, professional development, and research.